ZEEBONGO

THE
WACKY
WILD
ANIMAL
BUSINESS

by Frederik J. Zeehandelaar
as told to Paul Sarnoff

PRENTICE-HALL, INC.
ENGLEWOOD CLIFFS, NEW JERSEY

To Gertrude

ZEEBONGO: THE WACKY WILD ANIMAL BUSINESS
by Frederik J. Zeehandelaar as told to
Paul Sarnoff

ISBN-0-13-983957-7
Library of Congress Catalog Card Number: 74-132174
Printed in the United States of America T
Prentice-Hall International, Inc., London
Prentice-Hall of Australia, Pty. Ltd., Sydney
Prentice-Hall of Canada, Ltd., Toronto
Prentice-Hall of India Private Ltd., New Delhi
Prentice-Hall of Japan, Inc., Tokyo

Foreword

Of Fred J. Zeehandelaar, the story goes that he would telephone a zoo long-distance to enquire if his telegram had arrived. Asked which telegram, he replies: "The one which announced I would phone." It proves how thorough a man he is and, as he spells out in this book, that the art of communicating is his hobby.

A vital art indeed when it comes to the shipping of wild animals. A few years ago, the one Canadian railway company that serves all ten provinces accepted a load of zoo animals from a Prairie zoo for shipment along the major route to a point in southern Ontario. The animals, properly accommodated in crates and provided with food and water, were given a special car on a fast passenger train. The zoo was careful enough to notify the consignee of date and train number. On arrival at the consignee's place, the train did not have that car. The crew knew nothing, the train travelled on. That was that, as far as the railway company was concerned. Fortunately, the consignee had faith in the zoo's word and telephoned to ask what had gone wrong. Thereupon the zoo director prodded the railway officials into some action. They somehow established finally that the car with the animals stood on a siding in a lonely northern Ontario lumbermill town, left behind, forgotten. The animals were given fresh air and fresh water and made it to their destination, when the car was coupled to the next train that came along eastbound.

Communications, "nursing a shipment along" as Zeehandelaar calls it, is indeed an art, a most beneficial, even a crucial art when it comes to the survival of wild animals in transit. It avoids, or it relieves the suffering of animals, and in this all of us are interested who work with wild animals and love them.

Few people learn the art of world-wide animal swapping and shipping properly, just as only a few Zoo Directors are, in Zeehandelaar's opinion, well trained for their demanding job. I would like to say, however, in defence of my colleagues, that many have made their zoo job a lifetime obsession; several have worked their way up through the grades from starting points as zoo paperpickers, pony-ride hands or unpaid keeper-trainees. They do know the sexual dimorphism between the male and the female giant red kangaroo, and it happens rarely that a major zoo person complains to the supplier that a certain zebra stallion will not breed, when in fact it could not. Imagine the supplier's embarrassment, who knew that this zebra was a castrated one but had "forgotten" to mention it in the sale. I hurry to add that the supplier was not F. J. Z.

3

and that the Zoo Director has grown wise enough to laugh about the matter.

The wild animal trade is indeed wild and wacky. Many people have tried themselves in it, but few have had the financial, physical and mental stamina to endure. Small wonder then when such a person is not necessarily the world's smoothest diplomat. But it is fun to be with these extraordinary people, and highly informative to read the inside story of their existence.

On 14 October, 1970, I visited Hanover Zoo in West Germany, a zoo which has been almost totally rebuilt in the last few years. I was hosted by the two Hermann Ruhes, father and son, who operate the beautiful zoo under a contract with the city of Hanover. The Ruhe family has a tradition of international wild animal dealings. Emperors, circus dynasties, hobbyists and zoos the world over have been and are their customers. As much as they know the handling of captive wild animals, so they know the people who deal with animals. We were having lunch when somehow we talked of Fred J. Zeehandelaar. Hermann Ruhe, Sr. commented: "Ein kluger Mann!" (A wise-and-clever man.)

Good luck, fearless Fred, in your writing venture: Ad multa volumina! (May there be many volumes.)

Dr. Gunter Voss.

Gunter Voss, Dr. rer. nat
Director, Metropolitan Toronto Zoo
(now under construction)

President, American Association of
Zoological Parks and Aquariums

Preface

In the summer of 1967 I began to compile a "disaster calendar" for a Boston-based publisher. I had to supply facts about disasters for each day in the calendar. And in seeking leading calamities of the past I naturally turned to the *World Almanac.* Quite by chance I came across a headline stating that in 1966 the Bronx Zoo had purchased its most expensive wild animal, a baby male takin, for the seemingly stupendous sum of $16,000. In the fine print under this headline was the information that the zoo's purchase of one of the rarest of all living animals had been "engineered" by Fred J. Zeehandelaar, a New Rochelle, New York, wild animal dealer.

Spurred by irrepressible curiosity I immediately left home and drove off to the Bronx Zoo to feast my aging eyes on a single animal which cost as much as a new Rolls-Royce, F.O.B. the London docks. But seeing the takin wasn't as breathtaking an experience as I had imagined. Impulsively, I decided to look up the "genius" who had arranged for the sale of such an ugly animal at such a huge price. Then and there I drove a bit further north to New Rochelle in order to look up Mr. Zeehandelaar.

In retrospect, although the takin really didn't turn out to be a memorable experience, meeting Zeehandelaar resulted in indelible impact. This book is a result of that meeting.

Paul Sarnoff
Oceanside, New York

List of Illustrations

Contents

1.

A Heart Attack Business

Many books have been written about safaris, African hunting and adventure, zoos, and about people connected with animals. But to the best of my knowledge a book has never before been written about the wild animal business. This book is basically about the wild animal business—and mainly the business's suppliers, shippers, hunters, exporters and importers, zoo directors, zoological scientists, and all kinds of people desiring to buy wild animals for the purposes of exhibition, breeding, research, and promotion. Also included in this group are the people who finance wild animal deals, plus government officials and a host of other people involved in the various aspects of animal shipping and transportation.

Ned Payne, once one of America's most famous big game hunters, who has since reformed—and whose interest now is to preserve wildlife—says: "I have always been fascinated at how they ship big animals like hippos and elephants from one place to another. . . ." A similar aura of fascination has evidently pervaded newspaper and magazine articles for many years. But for me, the shipment of animals—large and small—is much more than a fascination. For me it is a dedicated business way of life. By definition, the wild animal business involves meeting the demands of a wide variety of persons and institutions. I have been so involved in this field during the past eighteen years that despite continuing and concomitant hazards the wild animal business has become an almost all-absorbing passion.

By way of introduction, I am Frederik J. Zeehandelaar. (The Frederik is spelled without the "c"; and what my middle initial means is nobody's business.) Voltaire believed "a bore is a person who tells everything"; lest I be called a bore I will reveal in this book only those things about the animal business readers ought to know.

This is also in accord with a well-remembered piece of advice from my father: "Life is a battle, bitter or friendly, but nevertheless a battle. Hide well your devices or others more lightfingered will carry away the fruits of victory." My father told me he acquired this bit of business wisdom while reading about the American sculptor then being acclaimed for his remarkable statue of General Sherman which still stands at the south end of Central Park in New York City. Like so many other Americans, I cannot now remember this sculptor's name, but I have never forgotten my father's advice and have practiced it diligently all my adult life.

For me the animal business is, at least on balance, a profitable one (no one lasts very long in modern business if profits are absent). I have very few competitors; the number of significant wild animal dealers in the United States today can be counted on one hand.

Without undue conceit, I believe I am one of America's largest *wholesale* wild animal dealers. Perhaps those better publicized people, like the man who used to be in downtown New York City and was known as "the Monkey King," should be called "retailers." You will not find me in the yellow pages of the telephone directory under "Animal Dealers" nor under "Birds," although I have probably imported more large birds—including penguins—than anybody else in America.

If anyone wants a *pet*—parrot, monkey, penguin, cockatoo, etc.—chances are that one of those retailers would get the order.

Exhibit of F.J. Zeehandelaar, Inc. in New York Hilton at Annual Convention of American Association for Laboratory Animal Science.

But when a Midwest zoo wishes to install a penguin collection for an aquarium, chances are that I will get the order. The following extract from a purchase order dated October 27, 1967, involving fifty-six penguins to be delivered by air in "two shipments" gives some clue to my wholesale stature:

Mr. Fred J. Zeehandelaar
F. J. Zeehandelaar, Inc.
New Rochelle, New York 10801

Dear Fred:

Thank you for your letter of October 12, in which you submitted quotations on penguins you can supply. We agree to purchase the following penguins from F. J. Zeehandelaar, Inc.:

20	King	@	$600 ea.	$12,000.
10	Rockhopper	@	450 ea.	4,500.
10	Blackfoot	@	300 ea.	3,000.
6	Gentoo	@	500 ea.	3,000.
10	Macaroni	@	450 ea.	4,500.
		TOTAL		$27,000.

This agreement is made with the following stipulations:

> No payment will be made for any bird until ten days after arrival.
>
> No payment will be made for any bird which is dead on arrival, or any bird which does not arrive in good condition and is not feeding. (By feeding, we mean that all birds will take fish from the hand. Not feeding means that birds refuse to eat and require netting and food forced into their mouths.) Birds in poor condition will not be accepted for payment until they are in good condition and feeding properly.
>
> You stated in your letter that the penguins from Antarctica will be transported by boat to Europe and will be held in the Hannover or Gelsenkirchen zoos for inspection before transportation to our zoo by air. We agree to this, but would specify that they not be flown to our zoo until we so authorize you; and we would also require that they be transported by air to our zoo in two shipments so that we do not have to adjust all the birds to our quarters at the same time.

Anyone who has had the least bit of experience with contracts will immediately see the risks I take. I had to pay for the birds at the time they were shipped to Hannover or Gelsenkirchen —and then sweat for my money until the zoo determined that the live penguins that managed to survive the trip ate "fish from the hand." Obviously, my profit on this 56-penguin deal depended upon the number of birds with good appetites. Penguins that died enroute, of course, were fully covered by insurance.

Among my more memorable wholesale imports of the past are 146 giant red kangaroos from Australia, 39 zebras from Africa, 89 wallabys from Australia, 35 African ostriches, 21 dromedary camels from Australia, and 14 elephants from India. One highly involved sale-and-swap transaction involving animal shipments to three continents brought the only male takin in captivity in the Western Hemisphere to the Bronx Zoo.

Arranging for animal importations of such magnitude takes a mountain of paperwork, many hours of planning, weeks and months of waiting—but most of all *effective communication.*

Emily Hahn, who watched my frenetic activity, once called me "communications crazy." Why? Because she was deeply impressed with the fact that within thirty seconds I can send messages from my New Rochelle office to a host of people scattered in almost every part of the world. Actually, the business of bringing large shipments of wild animals from their native lands to the United States could hardly be successfully accomplished were I unable to maintain orderly and almost instantaneous communication with key people around the globe.

To illustrate some complexities, traumas, and tribulations associated with my business triumphs, it should be noted that before any wild animals can be imported into the United States, I, as the importer, must obtain clearance from as many (at times) as five Federal agencies. I must also deal with shippers and with insurance companies. When the animals are finally released to my custody in the United States, before delivery to my customers arrangements must be made with airlines and trucking companies, and sometimes with railroads. In between these negotiations I try to keep the customer from losing his patience.

My customers' orders arrive at my office either by wire, by letter, by purchase order, or at times in the form of a lengthy and involved contract. Upon my agreement to fill these orders—and I have no desire to bag all the business in the wild animal world and so often turn down orders for unattainable animals or because other conditions of purchase or sale are untenable—I send back acceptances. After the arrival of the specified animals in this country, and after they have been cleared by the appropriate agencies, I deliver the creatures to my customers. Eventually, sometimes sooner, I get paid. And I then rush my recovered principal-plus-profit right down to the bank. That's the way it should be. For every American businessman should operate on two basic principles: (1) service and (2) profit. Although

I always attempt to render service, profit is often an uncertain and elusive end. Honestly, I often think I'm in a heart attack business.

A number of years ago a famous American circus sent me a bona fide purchase order for twelve dromedary camels. The purchase order arrived without a deposit. At that time I did not have too much experience with circuses, so I placed full confidence in the validity of the purchase order.

Four months later—and precisely on the day the boat bearing the camels approached the entrance of the New York harbor—I received a telegram from the circus canceling the order, due to lack of cash.

What would I do with twelve camels in New York City the next morning? Where could I board them until I found other buyers? How many zoos in the United States would even buy two camels, let alone twelve? Who could I call for help? Where should I start?

I did not sleep the entire night. Via telephone and telegraph I sought a miracle. It came at dawn when a Florida game farm offered to relieve me of my twelve-camel burden—but at a drastically reduced price.

In this case, the financial loss was not nearly as harrowing as the visions I conjured up during my sleepless night, as I imagined profit and principal vanishing with the dawn. Ever since then I do not accept purchase orders from *any* circus unless that piece of paper is accompanied by a substantial deposit.

On another occasion I received a letter from a zoo director in the United States to whom I had previously sold a pair of African rhinos. It seems one of the pair had died and the zoo director decided to obtain a new, young pair, provided I could successfully dispose of the old survivor. In other words, the zoo director, none too subtly, proposed I buy back the surviving rhino.

By good fortune I was able to obtain a prime pair of young African rhinos for eventual delivery to this zoo. And luckily

I was also able to sell the old rhino to a West Indies zoo. I did not examine the surviving rhino, since I relied entirely on the zoo director's word that the animal was in good condition. Putting the financial figures together I would come out with a profit for my trouble—if nothing went wrong.

In time the young rhinos arrived from Africa and were forwarded at my expense to the Midwest zoo. At the same time I wired the zoo director instructions to pack and ship (by truck) the surviving rhino to Miami, from which point I intended to fly the beast to the zoo in the West Indies—after a veterinarian had inspected it. To my dismay, the vet phoned me and reported that the rhino had a cataract in its left eye. He also confided that such a condition had to be of long standing. Obviously, the Midwestern zoo director knew his animal was flawed at the time he suggested the sale-and-swap. No sooner had the vet hung up than I contacted the director by phone and took him to task. He smoothly denied any knowledge of his rhino's deficiency.

What was I to do? Could I return the old rhino and reclaim the new pair? Could I ship a cataract-eyed rhino to the West Indies? Could I afford to have the many thousands of dollars already advanced for the young rhinos frozen by the Midwestern zoo while I fought them—possibly ineffectually—in the courts? Choking with anger I tried to make sense out of a sticky situation.

It didn't make economic sense to ship the old rhino back to the Midwest, because there was no guarantee the zoo director would take the beast back. Moreover, I hesitated to alienate him since the pair of young African rhinos I had imported were already at home in his zoo—and I was still awaiting payment. I did not dare risk flying the old rhino to the West Indies zoo in its present condition, because that zoo's director could hardly be expected to pay me for a defective animal when he had ordered one in good condition.

With my fingers literally crossed, I flew to the West Indies to explain the entire situation to the zoo director. Luckily, he was extremely sympathetic and agreed to accept the animal. But—and this becomes familiar—at a vast discount from the price originally agreed upon. My profit in this case, of course, was $000.

Don't think for a moment that I didn't cable the Midwestern zoo director to try to recover the discount given to the West Indies zoo director. But instead of money, the only thing I got back were wired cheers.

From this experience came another firm business policy. I decided then and there never to accept any animal from any zoo for resale or swapping purposes unless a competent veterinarian had first examined the animal on my behalf.

In all my arrangements for the shipment of animals, I am careful to insure my cargo. Although the premiums for this kind of insurance are indeed outrageous I can no more conduct my business without insurance protection than a New York driver can confidently operate his auto without liability insurance from some source. But when animals die and claims arise, the traumas that come with trying to collect from insurance companies are deep. Often these cases wind up in the courts.

Several years back I delivered two wolverines directly to a certain American zoo. The animals apparently arrived in good order and were thoroughly examined three days after their arrival by the zoo's veterinarian. They were given a clean bill of health and I was so notified by the zoo director who wrote me via airmail that the animals were "entirely acceptable."

Three days later both animals died. An autopsy revealed that the reason for their demise was "canine distemper." The zoo director, claiming that the cause of his animals' deaths was incubating inside the wolverines prior to their delivery to his zoo, withheld payment. We are now in the courts, where someday a judge and jury, who probably know nothing at all about wild animals, will decide whether or not Zeehandelaar should be paid.

Ignorance of the fine points about animal species is not confined to the nonprofessional public. It also crops up in the least expected places. A few years ago a zoo in the South ordered a pair of giant red kangaroos. Because we retain the privilege of partial delivery whenever an order for a pair of any animals is effected, we shipped the male kangaroo first, and a few weeks later, the female.

Shortly after arrival of this female kangaroo, the director sent me a letter that began:

> Dear Sir:
> The kangaroo arrived this morning and I was very disappointed in the animal. It is a mixture of blue and of grey with a very decided leaning to the grey. It does not make a pair very well with the red you sent before. . . .

To this letter of complaint I promptly wired:

> Please be advised only males are red, while females are grey. Refer to *Lydekkers' Royal Natural History*. Merry Christmas.

Naturally not all my days during the many years I have spent in the animal business are consistently harrowing or unprofitable. In fact there have been instances spiced with unexpected fun and profit. I can still vividly remember the largest profit, based on percentages, I ever made; and it came rather inadvertently from the sale of a frog.

There is a species of giant frog in Africa known as "Goliath." No frog of this species was exhibited in the United States from the onset of World War II—until after I filled an order for one in February 1961.

About six months before that eventful month, I received an inquiry from an American zoo asking for both the availability of such a frog and the price of its delivery to the zoo. To answer the inquiry I contacted a European supplier who relayed my request to Africa. The supplier was told that a frog could be caught and shipped "but the hunter had no idea of what the frog would cost to capture." And so the European supplier wired me that I could get delivery of such a frog but he didn't have the slightest notion as to what the amphibian would cost to be delivered into the United States. Without a precise knowledge of my cost I rather bullheadedly went ahead and calculated costs of shipping, insurance, and handling, and added on a nominal cost and profit. I then contacted the interested zoo and offered firmly one frog of the Goliath type in sound condition for $1,000—all the while hoping fervently the zoo would say "No."

To my surprise, the zoo director confirmed the order at that price; and I set the wires in motion which eventually would land the frog in our country.

After several maneuvers, international in scope, the frog arrived in the United States, and was rushed to the zoo. It never occurred to me to look through the packing case in which the frog was shipped for documents or papers, before shipping the box to the zoo. That was a mistake.

The day after the frog arrived at its new home I received a phoned complaint from the zoo director informing me that when he had removed the Goliath from his crate he had found tacked to its side a bill from the African supplier to the European supplier from whom I had ordered the frog. Although the African invoice was couched in local currency it wasn't too difficult for the zoo director to convert the figure into its value in dollars. This happened to come to precisely $65.

In retrospect, I can hardly blame this zoo director for feeling he had been gulled into paying $1,000 for a $65-frog. And at that time he vented his feelings rather forcibly on the telephone demanding a substantial deduction—or else.

Again. What was I to do? Obviously I had paid much more than $65, but the point of the entire matter is that at the time, I had committed myself to delivering a frog for which I had no earthly way of determining a price. On the other hand, if it had cost me more than $1,000 I would have made good on the delivery and, swallowing hard, taken my loss. Yet how was I to handle this director's complaint diplomatically and ~~still~~ stick to the principles of doing business fairly and properly?

In reality my only excuses were: (1) I did not negotiate directly with the primary supplier in Africa and my European intermediary was entitled to a profit, (2) shipping and insurance costs were so-much and so-much based on a $1,000 evaluation, (3) a certain amount of my money was being tied up—and losing possible bank interest—while the zoo held up payment, and (4) no matter what else was to be considered we had made a firm contract: I had kept my side of the bargain—and would have kept it at no matter the cost or loss—while the zoo director was reneging.

In the end, I insisted upon payment in full. And eventually I did receive full payment. But while this turned out to be the most profitable wild animal deal I have ever made, it could hardly be classed as successful public relations.

My most significant exploit in the field of successful public relations involved the delivery of a male takin to the Bronx Zoo —and not only because it landed me in the *World Almanac* (1967).

In 1959 the Bronx Zoo became host to a female takin (pronounced TAH-kin), one of the world's rarest living animals, representing a breed rapidly facing extinction. Imagine a quadruple cross between a musk-ox, a Shensi-goat, an American bison, and an African antelope—and an idea of a takin's appearance begins to form. Like Paiute ponies, takins have Roman noses ending in black nostrils and muzzles. The female flaunts a delicately curved pair of black horns not much longer than the tusks of a wart hog, while the male takin waves a wicked pair of black horns which grow from its forehead on a rakish angle— and are at least a foot long. The stocky bodies of these "clumsily built" creatures are broad at the shoulders, tapering finely down at the hind quarters, not unlike the bison. A leading zoologist claims this species reflects "physical characteristics of cattle, musk-oxen and goat-antelopes." The coat of the female is

U-Mishmi—male Takin at Bronx Zoo

usually a dark dun color, while that of the male is more golden.
Down the backs of both male and female takins run lines of
frizzly black hair. Although cumbersome in appearance, takins
in their native habitat are quite agile, and can move incredibly
swiftly, when necessary.

   Living precariously on the high slopes of the Himalayas in the
region encompassing Burma and the lower part of China, takins
favor extremely rough country. During the day they lurk in dense
thickets of dwarf bamboo and rhododendron on impenetrable
mountains, eight-to-fourteen thousand feet above sea level,

mountains where steady rains during a good part of the year make the tracking of takins by civilized hunters quite unbearable. Highly elusive, takins are almost never taken into captivity and are hardly ever seen during daylight hours by natives of the area they inhabit.

During the day, takins wisely lurk deep inside their dense thickets, living in winter on bamboo shoots, and grazing during the summer on the grassy slopes at dusk and at dawn. The slightest noise sends these sensitive animals scooting along paths of their own making, back into their thickets. Burmese and Chinese prize these beasts for food. To them takins are considered "yeh nin" (wild cattle) and predators behind the Bamboo Curtain have virtually decimated takin herds completely. Moreover, because these "goat-antelopes" conceive only one offspring at a time they are rapidly becoming extinct. It is exceedingly ironic that this seemingly useless creature, which hides all day and is fated to wind up in a deadfall spear-trap or snare, has become one of the most sought-after zoo-prizes in the animal kingdom.

It is not so accidental that after six long years of searching, the Bronx Zoo relied upon me to provide them with a male takin so that they could hopefully breed takins in the Bronx and thus save the species.

In 1966 a friend told me that the zoo in Rangoon, Burma, had a male takin less than a year old which they would consider exchanging for other animals. I wasn't interested in the kind of deal which would involve me in sending animals from Africa to Rangoon and then swapping them for the single takin that would be shipped to New York. Obviously, the least complicated deal would have been cash. So I offered the Rangoon Zoo all kinds of monetary inducements—but the answer came back on wires that read *no.* In the end the only way I could get delivery of the takin from Rangoon was first to ship them, in exchange, two giraffes and four zebras from Africa.

Based on an estimate of my costs to bring the giraffes and zebras from Africa to Rangoon and subsequently to ship the takin from Rangoon to the Bronx—insuring and paying for feeding and care of the animals all the while—I quoted the zoo an offer of $16,000 for the takin, and again fervently hoped they would say no. To my chagrin they accepted the offer and ordered the takin.

And then I began to sweat. The zoo's terms of purchase, dated January 11, 1966, were:

The purpose of this note is to confirm our order for a male Burmese Takin (*Budorcas t. taxicolor*), approximately eight to nine months of age on December 4, 1965. It is our understanding that you will deliver this animal to the Bronx Zoo in good health and condition, guaranteed for thirty days, for $16,000. We understand, further, that this animal will be transferred to the U.S. for quarantine in March 1966. Our agreement to purchase is limited to 1966 and to this particular animal.

To further understand the complexities and the dangers to me— financially, that is—the zebras and giraffes had to be paid for and delivered to Rangoon before that zoo would release its male takin. Thereafter I would have to ship the beast by plane to Hamburg, Germany, where it would be in quarantine for sixty days; and then by freighter to New York City, where the animal would be taken to the Department of Agriculture Quarantine Station in Clifton, New Jersey, for the next thirty days, before being released to the Bronx Zoo. What would I do if the zebras and giraffes died before reaching Rangoon? And if they did arrive in good condition, what would happen if the takin died during its travels and quarantine periods? Just the protection of life insurance on the animals wasn't enough, for in the case of this male takin the Bronx Zoo's instructions specifically said: "Our agreement to purchase is limited to 1966 and to this particular animal."

Luckily, U-mishmi, the male takin, survived his travail from Rangoon to the Bronx (via Hamburg and Clifton); and luckily the zebras and giraffes were in good order on arrival at Rangoon;

and most fortunately for me the Bronx Zoo found no fault with their takin, paying for it after 30-days insurance had elapsed.

Zeehandelaar, Inc. probably is the only firm in the world that could have successfully effected such a complicated deal. To make the necessary arrangements I had, of course, to rely on trusted people in Europe, Africa, and Asia. I had to mollify and satisfy international authorities as to the origin of this takin, and nurse the entire transaction *every* step of the way. It seems, therefore, that the first qualification for being a successful wild animal dealer today is to be a great arranger.

2.
Makings of an Animal Dealer

I was born three days before Christmas, 1917, in Amsterdam, the Netherlands. Anyone who has ever visited Amsterdam knows why this wonderful place is called "the Venice of the North." Semicircular canals (grachten) crossed by transverse ones divide the entire city into a series of islands connected by four hundred bridges. Because Amsterdam lies below sea level and the ground is generally soft and boggy, nearly all Amsterdam houses are built upon wooden piles.

My father was a physician, and we lived in a large house on the Prinsengracht. My father was a general practitioner, and he was also a patriot: At the time I was born he was on active duty as a reserve medical officer. During World War I the Netherlands was not at war, but was merely mobilized, so my father served safely through this war with the rank of captain.

Two-and-a-half years after my birth another male Zeehandelaar (meaning "sea trader") arrived, and this was the extent of my family. As the oldest son it was foreordained that I follow in my father's footsteps. And from the time of my first understanding until my seventeenth birthday it was generally accepted by all in my family that I would become a physician.

But after I entered the university I discovered I did not have the patience to study. I could not sit for hours and hours reading books. Yet obediently I bent to the task for two-and-one-half years—until one day in 1938 I decided I had had enough. I decided to cut my parental cord and go out into the working world to earn some of my own money. Having made such a decision, I abruptly quit the university. Much to my father's disappointment I went to work in the office of an Amsterdam pharmaceutical factory owned by M.J. Lewenstein.

At that time, the Lewenstein works happened to be a large and active pharmaceutical factory on the Continent. As I worked away in the office I gained great—and as it later turned out, invaluable—experience in correspondence involving international sales and shipments. I also became known to Mr. Lewenstein, whom I always greeted courteously each morning as he arrived at the office.

In 1939 the black shadow of World War II shrouded the horizon and again the Netherlands mobilized. By dropping out of the university I had lost my student deferment, so I was compelled to leave Lewenstein to become "conscripted" into the Netherlands Army. But my father, who had been recalled as a colonel, intervened and I was sent to Officers' Candidate School, in the fall of 1939.

The school was located in Haarlem, about ten miles west of Amsterdam, and it was there that I successfully became an officer. But during May 1940, the Netherlands capitulated to the Nazis in less than a handful of fighting days; and Hitler's hordes swarmed into the country. By the end of May, the victorious Germans had demobilized the Dutch army, keeping career soldiers and senior officers as prisoners of war, and sending conscripts home.

I never saw my father again. Freedom was finished. In no time at all the Netherlands became incorporated into the Third Reich. I could not remain at home and watch my mother's anguish. Nor could I work at one job, or even sit still for a minute. Some internal force seemed to push me into movement. And so I left

Amsterdam to travel all over the country, trying to make my
meager ends meet by peddling accident-and-health insurance—
with emphasis on war-damage insurance.

At that time, of course, I knew nothing about either selling
or the insurance business; but a kindly relative on my mother's
side took me on and gave me the chance to learn the business.
I was soon bored by the insurance business and took a position
with a wholesale textile firm.

I did not go back to the Lewenstein firm for several
understandable reasons. Mr. Lewenstein, a great enemy of the
Germans, was Jewish. Wisely, in 1940, he had fled the country
and obtained refuge in the United States. In the meantime his
great works was being operated for the benefit of the Nazis.
The pharmaceuticals were being produced exclusively for the use
of the Germans, and there was no assurance as to what kind of
reception an ex-Dutch Army officer would receive if he applied
to the new owners for his old job.

In 1942 the situation in the Netherlands became almost
unbearable for ex-members of the Netherlands Army, so my
brother and I decided to leave the country. We wanted to escape
to England, where remnants of the Dutch Army attempted to
form a Netherlands Brigade.

Someday, in another book, I might fully describe the details of
our harrowing flight from under Nazi boots. But for this book
it is sufficient to note that the "short walk" from Amsterdam to
England took us *fourteen* months to accomplish. By walking—
and intermittently hitch-hiking—we traversed Belgium, France,
Switzerland, Spain, and Portugal. We even managed to
successfully cross the demarcation line between occupied and free
France.

In the process we used forged papers, false documents,
passports, etc., all the while relying heavily upon the kindness of
strangers. During our fourteen-month "trek" we were jailed by
both friends and enemies no less than twenty-one times. Because

of this we landed in prisons, war camps, and similar unappetizing "hostelries." We spent periods as short as one night and as long as three months in these horrible places.

But little did I realize as I struggled to find freedom that these harrowing experiences would stand me in good stead when handling bureaucratic problems I would later encounter in my wild animal business.

Eventually—and just like in the movies—we managed to arrive safely in England in May 1943.

My brother was conscripted into the Netherlands Overseas Forces, and went off to Australia, while I joined the Netherlands Brigade as a 2nd Lieutenant, motor transport officer. The Netherlands Brigade, of course, was part of the British Army and was preparing for the invasion of Continental Europe. It wasn't too long after I became a motor transport officer that I was promoted to 1st Lieutenant.

One of the first things "Leftenant" Zeehandelaar did was put himself into the hospital. I mention this because I believe this is the only case on record where a motor transport officer drove his own ambulance to the hospital.

The accident occurred while I was driving a jeep, but also imagining I was piloting a plane. The jeep flipped over—and my days of wild driving were finished. I dragged myself out from under the jeep—bleeding about the face and head, and bruised all over. Not trusting the only available ambulance driver (and not relishing the thought of having a second accident) I commandeered an ambulance and drove myself off to the base hospital.

My wounds healed quickly, and the following summer the Allied Invasion began. By winter I was once again back in the Netherlands attached to the Canadian Army. Coming home turned out to be a traumatic experience. My mother and most of my relatives had been "liquidated," so there was really nothing for me to come back to. Sadly, I returned to London.

In 1946 we were told that those who took part in the liberation of the Netherlands could emigrate, at army expense, to any country in the world, provided they themselves could arrange for civil immigration.

To me this news heralded a golden opportunity to visit the United States. I wanted to visit the United States primarily for three reasons:

1. I wanted to experience something entirely new and I wanted to forget the loss of my family in the Netherlands.
2. My old boss, Mr. Lewenstein, was in the United States. I had always admired him and thought I could go back into the pharmaceutical business with his help.
3. Even if I didn't desire to settle down in the United States for the rest of my life, I realized this was probably the only opportunity I would ever have to see this great country at somebody else's expense.

And so I decided to come to the United States at the expense of the Netherlands Army. This turned out to be easier said than done.

In the first place, army rules dictated that anyone traveling to another country at army expense had to travel under army orders, and remain in full uniform at all times during the trip. But American laws do not permit immigrants to enter the United States as long as they are members of a foreign armed force. This seemingly unsolvable dilemma probably caused my metamorphosis into a "great arranger."

I arranged with friends to be discharged on a given day from the Netherlands Army. Bearing my discharge papers on that day I visited the American consul and obtained the necessary papers for admission into the United States. Immediately after receiving the proper papers I had myself recalled into the Netherlands Army so that I could receive the necessary movement order (papers to travel). Forthwith the Netherlands Army arranged for me to travel (not quite in luxury) from London to Montreal on a Royal Air Force bomber.

I arrived in Montreal in June 1946, and immediately had to satisfy Canadian officials at the airport that it was legally permissible for me to visit that country on the way to the United States. I then went off to arrange for my immigration entry into the United States. Although I did not wear a civilian suit, but still wore my Netherlands Army uniform, I really didn't expect any trouble.

How smart was that wise fellow who once said, "I never worry about the things I know. It's the things I don't know that make me worry." Little did I realize I would have plenty to worry about after I arrived at the American Consulate in Montreal.

It seems I had violated one little rule. A spokesman told me that all prospective immigrants must travel to the United States on such conveyances that guarantee that if the immigrant is not admitted he will be carried back without charge to where he came from by said conveyances. In other words, carriers bringing immigrants into the United States must be signatories to agreements to take immigrants back if found unacceptable. Since I had arrived in North America on an RAF bomber, I had traveled on a carrier which had not signed such an agreement with the United States. And until such an agreement was signed and delivered to the immigration authorities I was forever barred from immigrating into the United States. How do they sing it in song? "So near and yet so far?"

Assuredly this was the greatest challenge of my life in the arrangements department. My seemingly insuperable task was to get the RAF to sign a paper saying they would gladly ship me back to London, Amsterdam, or Jibroo if I turned out to be unacceptable to American authorities. And Canadian informants immediately told me that the RAF had never in all its exciting history signed such a paper.

The fact that I am writing this book in America is proof positive that I was able to commit the RAF to such a signed agreement with the U.S.A. And on June 7, 1946, I stepped down from a Colonial Airlines plane at La Guardia Field, in New York

City. I could hardly believe I had made it, but here I was, at last, in the United States.

No sooner had I landed in New York than I went to visit Mr. Lewenstein. There is a strangely compelling camaraderie between people born in the same country, who later find themselves living in another. This is especially so when one comes from such a small country as the Netherlands. Mr. Lewenstein and I became fast friends—a friendship that sadly ended all too soon upon his passing some years ago. And it was at the Lewensteins that I first met my wife, Gertrude.

Not so oddly, it turned out that Gertrude's original home had been in Amsterdam, some three blocks from my father's house. Somehow I had never met her in Holland; but I couldn't help noticing that this dark-haired vivacious girl, who when I met her worked for the Netherlands Shipping Commission, was quite animated and intelligent during the discussions and the arguments we used to have at the Lewensteins'. Looking back, I realize how much fun we used to have simply arguing.

Very often the conversation at the Lewensteins' turned to manner and methods of extracting some of our small savings still held in Holland. At that time, no one was permitted to take out Netherlands currency and exchange it for American dollars. At

Mr. M. J. Lewenstein

one of these discussions Gertrude made some extremely intelligent suggestions which made a lasting impression upon me because they were: (1) from a woman, and (2) workable and correct.

Thereafter our friendship flowered very quickly—and we decided to be married quietly. We first met in September 1946; in January 1947, we decided to get married; and precisely on August 10, 1947, we did just that. During the past—and wonderful—years with Gertrude she has given me many things, including two sons: Eric and David. Gertrude, in addition to her busy home schedule, has her own hobby and business involving cats. Since I do not wish to ruin any book she might someday write on her own experiences, I will just say that in our home there are normally six living cats, hundreds of cat statuettes, cat pictures and cat paintings—and one of the world's most extensive libraries strictly devoted to cats.

It has been said that a wife and children are hostages to fortune. Frankly I believe this thought to be sheer bunk. Although I run my own business, Gertrude has been, all through the years, a valued friend and advisor—and has greatly contributed to whatever success or fortune is now mine. I do not know what would have become of me if it wasn't for her.

Shortly after I arrived in New York City in 1946, I went to visit an import-export corporation, which shall hereinafter be termed the "downtown corporation," whose principal stockholders were once patients of my beloved father. Fortunately these people had left the Netherlands in the early 1930's and so were firmly established in the United States long before the Nazis devastated our once beautiful country. I visited these kind people and applied for a job. It was given to me at once, and I found myself working for a firm that was in a fascinating and diversified business. One of its divisions imported and exported metals and metal products. Another division involved itself with chemicals. Still another, textiles and general merchandise. At first, I worked in the chemical-export department, until 1949 when the pound sterling was first devalued and all exports from the United States became excessively expensive to countries whose currency was devalued in the wake of the British debacle.

Then I was switched to a traveling job and found myself sent to Haiti for copper, to Korea for tungsten, to Japan for crude iodine, to Spain for potash, and to other far-off places for various commodities. During my travels I found that the fastest, and yet most economical, method of communication with my wife was by cable. Because cables sent to an established cable address (usually an initialism or acronym) are less expensive than those sent to a spelled-out street address, I decided to acquire a cable address of my own. I hit upon the word "bongo."

At that time I had no idea I would ever be in the wild animal business; nor was I aware then as I am today that a bongo is an extremely rare African antelope. But I lit on the word "bongo" as my own cable address simply because at that time there was a very popular song flooding the airwaves that went something like "Bongo, Bongo, in the Congo." But the cable office in New York told me that all cable addresses in its area must have at least *seven* letters, and that Bongo, containing five, was unpermissible. The cable address agency kindly suggested, however, that I add the three letters starting my last name to make a highly euphemistic *Zeebongo*.

Never let it be said that Fred Zeehandelaar doesn't act quickly when he hears good advice. Immediately I said, "OK. *Zeebongo* it is." It has been my cable address ever since.

Years later a firm aspiring to be my competitor opened in another area of the United States—one in which a five-letter cable name is permissible—and to my chagrin they promptly filed for (and were permitted to use) the cable name: *Bongo.* I felt—and still do feel—that this is quite unfair. Who knows, some people might mistakenly do business with the "bongo" people, thinking they are doing business with *me.*

In any event, my cable address, *Zeebongo,* is today famous all over the animal export-import world.

3.
Experimental Years

Actually my first involvement in the wild animal business came unexpectedly in 1951, while I was still working for the downtown corporation. One of our overseas customers, short of cash because of a devaluation, wrote and asked if we would accept some snakes and rhesus monkeys in payment for our products. I answered in the affirmative, and my whole life changed with that single correspondence.

The customer who offered my company the snakes and monkeys happened to be a dealer of Madagascar cloves, based in the Malagasy Republic. At the time he offered us rhesus monkeys I did not know that that genus is not native to the Malagasy Republic, but rather is native to India. But I was so eager to plunge into a new area of marketing that this made no difference to me. All I could see at the time was the challenge of something new to sell.

Based on the cost to my company of these rhesus monkeys offered by the Malagasy supplier, I wrote to every zoo in the United States, to the universities, and to the research institutes, offering rhesus monkeys F.O.B. New York City at $96 each. Almost holding my breath, I anxiously watched the mail for favorable results of my first wild animal marketing campaign.

Alas, the few replies I received indicated I was crazy. But some respondents were kind enough to point out that although I didn't belong in the wild animal business the going price for rhesus monkeys then was about $36. By that time I had learned that this species of monkey comes from India and that our Malagasy contact was acting as a high-priced middleman.

Never let it be said Fred Zeehandelaar is either a slow thinker or lacks intestinal fortitude, sometimes called "guts." I immediately shot out another letter to everybody who received my first letter about monkeys, saying that my first letter had contained a typographical error: The price was not $96; but rather $34.

Shortly thereafter I received several orders from research institutions—and letters from zoos and game farms asking me if I could supply any other animals besides monkeys and snakes. But the genuine bonus came when I received a surprise visit from the owner of an American game farm who for this book's purpose assumes the alias, Jim Jones.

A week or so after I had mailed out my second letter about rhesus monkeys, a dynamic gentleman appeared in the office of the downtown corporation and asked for me. "My name is Jim Jones," he began abruptly, "and I want to tell you, you don't know anything at all about animals."

To this I retorted, "Pardon me, but did you come here to insult me?"

"Oh no. You see I know all about animals, but nothing about the mechanics of financing and shipping them. I thought that since you know nothing about animals, but much about foreign trade, we could work together."

Jim Jones seemed both disarming and intriguing at the same time. Instead of throwing him bodily out of my office (my first impulse, of course), I reacted like a meek schoolboy facing his teacher and asked, "What do you want me to do?"

He promptly said, "I want you to import for me twenty zebras. If the price is acceptable, I will give your firm a profit of 25 percent above the total cost delivered to my game farm."

Little did I know what Jones had in mind, but twenty zebras—figuring vaguely what decent domestic horses bring—sounded like a large order. I accepted his proposition and plunged into expediting the order with more excitement than I can ever remember.

To find twenty zebras, I wrote long letters to every American embassy in Africa for the names of wild animal hunters and suppliers. Eventually I received some 200 letters in reply. One of these letters was from a misplaced Swiss citizen located in Arusha, Tanganyika (now Tanzania) who quoted me a price of $262 each for twenty zebras F.O.B. Mombasa.

I relayed this information to Jones and he agreed to pay my firm as soon as the animals arrived. On the strength of this, I went ahead and cabled the Swiss supplier in Arusha to go ahead and forward the twenty zebras. He promptly cabled back asking if I could use forty zebras instead of twenty. I called Jones and he readily agreed to take the forty. So I cabled back to Arusha and the deal was set.

I was as excited as a kid waiting for Christmas. Questions zipped continuously through my mind. How would the animals be packed? Could they survive a long ocean trip? What would the costs be? for feeding? for freight? for insurance? What had to be done after the ship arrived? How long and how costly would the quarantine be? As I struggled to find the answers to all these questions, more than once the nagging question of how long it would take Jones to pay for his order returned to pester me.

The doubts and the misgivings and the questions were crowded from my mind on the morning of June 30, 1952, when the *SS Robin Trent* docked at the foot of Columbia Street, Brooklyn.

In just moments, the normally drab waterfront was magically transformed as the colorful animals were put ashore for the truck trip to the quarantine station. Of the forty animals loaded aboard the ship at Mombasa, only one had succumbed to the rigors of

The "Downtown Corporation's" first shipment of 39 Zebras (*The Port of New York Authority*)

the 43-day crossing. Solemnly, the ship's master told me that this zebra had died of a heart attack, and had been buried at sea.

When the excitement of my first international transaction in the wild animal business wore off, I began to calculate the real cost. The total ran precisely $786 per animal, which, of course, included my firm's 25 percent profit. I presented Jones with a bill for approximately $30,000 and asked for a check.

No such luck.

Mr. Jones revealed that he didn't have $30,000 cash readily available, that the prosperity of his business depended upon the weather, and that therefore he hoped it wouldn't rain over the weekend so that many people would visit his game farm.

To those companies whose shares are listed for trading on the New York Stock Exchange, $30,000 may not seem to be a lot of money; but for the firm for which I slaved it represented a sizable sum. Persistently, and probably forcibly, I insisted that Jones show good faith—in the form of cash.

He managed to come up with a check of $5,000—with the proviso that if the weather were fair for the coming weekend he would produce another $5,000 that Monday. My superior in the downtown corporation was livid. But there really wasn't much either of us could do—except pray for fair weather.

It took Jones many weeks to finally make payment in full. It seemed that this zebra deal was to be the first and the last wild animal trade in which I would ever be involved.

For the next few months I completely lost interest in the animal business and devoted myself to fostering the export of chemicals and the import of spices, hedging commodity-exchange transactions, and worrying about how I could successfully market low-grade copper ore from a mine in Haiti.

To my complete surprise, Jones again approached our busy firm. I had imagined that anyone who had financially hung up an importer for so long a time would be reluctant to try again. But I didn't know Jones very well at the time. He offered to buy 146 giant red kangaroos on the same basis as he had bought the 39 zebras. To my further amazement, my boss said, "Go ahead." In retrospect, I imagine he figured that even if we waited three months for our money we were earning 100 percent on an annual basis at the rate of 25 percent profit per quarter, so the incentive obviously was there to take risks.

But shortly after we gave the order to a firm in Australia and the 146 kangaroos were being processed for shipment to the States, we caught on to what Jones was doing.

Some—if not all—of the zebras imported for $786 through the use of our facilities and our credit were being resold to zoos for $1,500 each. And it became perfectly obvious that Jones intended to market the kangaroos at twice their cost—again using our credit to earn 100 percent profit at the same time that we were earning only 25 percent. And what made this even more

financially insulting was that Jones was doing this without
laying out a dollar or a dime of his own funds! Not a bad deal
in any market game.

After some serious consultation with my superior we decided
that the downtown firm would enter the wild animal business as
principals—and not as Jones's middlemen. Today, Jim Jones
operates one of the largest, most prosperous, and most
popular game farms in the world. But much of his success
should be attributed to the financial assistance of the downtown
corporation, and to my own efforts involving letters of credit, bills of
lading, cables, phone calls, coordination of agencies and
shippers, etc.

Shortly after the downtown corporation decided to venture into
the wild animal business as principals, I decided it would be
prudent to secure a readily available—and safe—haven for the
large quantities of animals we intended to import so that they
could be kept in stock until sold to zoos, collectors, and circuses.
But little did I realize that by acting in this prudent, logical
fashion I was about to create one of the biggest business mistakes
I ever inadvertently initiated.

On behalf of my firm I entered into an agreement with the
McKee Jungle Gardens at Vero Beach, Florida, to provide a
shelter for the animals we intended to import. In exchange for
supplying the animal specimens to be viewed at the gardens, we
would receive a fair share of the admission money. But in the
meantime, we would be compelled to feed and maintain our
animals.

No sooner had we concluded the arrangement with the McKee
Gardens than we set out with zest to populate Florida with
African animals. Our compound had a myriad of elephants,
giraffes, lions, tigers, jaguars, assorted rare birds, snakes, and
monkeys. Everything alive was for sale—except the human
beings. The trouble was if we stocked penguins, the zoos needed
ocelots. If we stocked rhinos, the zoos wanted hippos. And so it
went. In the meantime, the animals were eating up a fortune—

and many were dying. To make matters worse, the caretakers hired
to look after the animals were inexperienced and unskilled; this
caused complications resulting in bad publicity.

For example, on Sunday evening, May 16, 1954, a one-ton,
seven-year-old female elephant named Margarete broke her chains
and departed from the compound—without notice. When her
departure was discovered the following morning, the compound
manager took off to track down the runaway elephant. But he had
as little chance of finding Margarete in the Florida jungle as he
would have had finding his wife in Macy's the Saturday before
Christmas.

Margarete in the interim was off making headlines and amassing
allegations of damage. After a fruitless search of some thirty
hours, the disheveled Gardens manager called in the Coast Guard.
Immediately this efficient service lofted a helicopter to track down
the lumbering beast, who could, of course, be a danger to life and
limb if she so desired. It was the first time in history that the
Coast Guard went out on an elephant safari, and as to be expected
they were unsuccessful. On Wednesday, a fisherman on the Indian
River almost fell out of his boat watching Margarete sun herself
on a sandbar in the middle of the river. Having read of the
runaway in the papers, the fisherman headed for shore and the
nearest telephone. Many hours later Margarete docilely
accompanied her mahout back to the compound, without incident.

But the legal claims that arose from this beast's two- or
three-day escapade were incredible. One farmer reported the
elephant had trampled his vegetable garden, had ruined a
clothesline, and had destroyed a barbed-wire fence. Another
farmer reported his cow had died of a heart attack when she saw
the massive beast. And there were other seemingly fatuous claims.
Somehow we restored happiness in a disturbed area, but it took
a good deal of money to soothe things after our elephant's escape.

One day the manager of the compound got a brainstorm. He
suggested that since we were in the animal importing business
and the animal attraction business it would be nice to be in the

animal mail-order business, too. He suggested we start with baby caymans, about the size of a person's hand.

I concluded a very satisfactory deal with one of the country's largest mail-order houses and they inserted an ad for the baby caymans in their catalogue. The orders came down upon our office like the proverbial flood. The mail-order house, of course, took no risk on shipping expense, since it used our facilities in Florida for drop shipment. And even though the mail firm received payment in advance, it didn't make payment to us until we had actually made shipment. Soon we found ourselves up to both elbows in woe.

Baby caymans have sharp teeth, and it doesn't take very long for these babies to become bigger—with their teeth becoming much more dangerous in the process. Soon we had a flood of returns from indignant people who demanded their money back from the mail-order house. We were even threatened with lawsuits from parents who had bought the little critters for their children and were highly upset by the resulting bloody fingers and arms. Financially, this mail-order venture turned out to be a debacle. But were we deterred?

Since burros sell for about $8 south of the border, we went into another mail-order deal with the same giant mail-order house to drop-ship Mexican burros to American customers. After calculating the costs of shipping, duty, feed, insurance, and acquisition to be $28 per animal, we quoted the burros to the mail-order house at $42 each. The mail-order firm promptly began to retail the animals for $85 each. The sale of these asses caused such a sensation, the story made *Life* Magazine.

Oddly enough, many orders for these burros came from Americans located near the Mexican border, where for a little time and trouble, plus duty, they could be bought for under $20. To this day I cannot help but marvel at the person who can buy something close at hand for less than $20, and pays $85 for the same thing because the item is advertised by a firm in Chicago.

For our $14 profit per burro we had plenty of unexpected problems. Naturally we shipped the animals North from Mexico in freight cars, with cardboard tags noting the names and addresses of the recipients attached to the necks of the burros. But the burros took a liking to the cardboard tags and made a habit of eating them before reaching their destination. When the animals arrived at the terminal for transfer to their rightful owners, the railroad people couldn't tell who was supposed to get the asses.

Meanwhile, we, as the drop shipper, were responsible for feeding and maintaining the burros. And the added costs of doing this while frantically tracking down the rightful owners turned out to be staggering.

To avoid additional trouble from the cardboard tags we changed to metal tags, which the burros couldn't eat. But we found troubles elsewhere. The mail-order house wound up with all kinds of complaints: The burros were not the right size, or the right sex, or the right color. Some owners complained long after they had received the asses that the animals were not tame, or that they messed up the gardens, or that they bit their children. Needless to say, we were not long in the mail-order business, since we didn't enjoy refunding money.

But the crowning trauma came when an Indian supplier wired us a firm offer of a giant panda at an unbelievably low price. I promptly wired our acceptance, and just as promptly offered the panda to American zoos on a first-come-first-served basis at $15,000. I received three firm orders and wired the Indian supplier, asking if he could ship three pandas instead of one.

To my dismay he wired back that he could not ship three animals—and if I wanted the one panda my firm would have to commit itself to the purchase of $50,000 worth of additional animals. We wired a confirmation to one zoo and cancellation to the other two. At the same time we went ahead and ordered, among other animals, giant tortoises, elephants, and cranes to make up the additional $50,000 shipment demanded by this nefarious dealer. In the meantime, we opened a general letter of credit for this dealer with a Bombay Bank, but made it negotiable *only after* the panda had been shipped *to us.*

Neither the panda nor any of the other animals were ever shipped. Evidently the giant panda "ran away." This aborted attempt to swindle my firm came a cropper when the restricted letter of credit was issued with the one condition the dealer couldn't cope with. The main reason I took this precaution is that I had learned there are some three hundred wild animal dealers in India, but only two or three are *real* dealers. The rest are questionable brokers. Of course, as an outcome of this experience, relations were temporarily strained between the downtown corporation and the zoo which had expected the panda but had never received delivery.

All during the exciting years of my apprenticeship in the wild animal business, my superior patiently put up with the mistakes, the traumas, and the losses. The reason for his liberal attitude is obvious: Despite my early inexperience and occasional bungling, my animal importation project had proved profitable. But suddenly, in 1956, the managers of the downtown corporation decided its capital could be put to better use than feeding animals that zoos were not eager to buy—animals eating up company profits in the McKee Jungle Gardens.

At about the same time, I reasoned that if I were in my own business—with low overhead and systematic service—I could make a stunning monetary success from this business. Moreover, much of the profits generated from animal importation and supply from 1952 through 1956 had already been dissipated by other divisions of the downtown corporation. And so I decided to chance it on my own.

If I had been single at the time of my decision, my choice would have been quite easy to make. But at the time I was married and the father of two small sons. My responsibility for my loved ones made me hesitate a long time when deciding whether I should abandon the security of working with the firm I had been with for so many years for the insecurity of trying to make it on my own. After talking it through with my beloved wife I walked into my boss's office one day and told him I was leaving. I also told him I intended to go into the wild animal business on my own.

At this he grew greatly disturbed, pointing out that he was saddled with some four hundred animals and birds in the compound at Vero Beach, which even at bargain prices were worth $25,000. And he demanded I relieve him of this financial burden before I left. Although I was not legally obligated to relieve him of anything at all, I decided to make a deal for the animals in Florida. But this required capital, one commodity I did not have enough of at the time.

Once again, just like Blanche in Tennessee Williams' *Streetcar Named Desire,* I "depended upon the kindness of strangers. " But my benefactor in this instance was no stranger. He was Mr. Lewenstein, my old friend and employer. This very kind man risked the $5,000 I needed to start off on my own. And at last I was a full-fledged wild animal dealer able to do business as I saw fit.

4.
Belated Reflections

In 1957 I was forty—and on my own. There was no time to look back; the future beckoned invitingly—and threateningly. For the next ten years I didn't stop running as I created one of the largest wholesale wild animal businesses in the world. The secret of my success was a combination of things: (1) I created a systemized approach to matching wild animal buyers and sellers all over the world, (2) I created a communications network between hunters, suppliers, shippers, freight forwarders, etc., which has worked fantastically well, and (3) my wife put up with the concomitant inconveniences without too much complaining.

Frankly I probably would never have taken the time or the trouble to record some of the highlights in my hectic life as a wild animal dealer if it were not for an unexpected visitor in August 1967.

On a typical dog-day in that month I happened to be talking on two phones at the same time—to a zoo director on the West Coast, and to a primary source in Europe—when my office door flew open and a bulky, blue-eyed, beardless version of Orson Welles waddled up to my desk and waited for me to finish. As soon as I cradled the phones he asked, "Mr. Zeehandelaar?" And I answered, "What can I do for you?" And he shot back, "I'd like

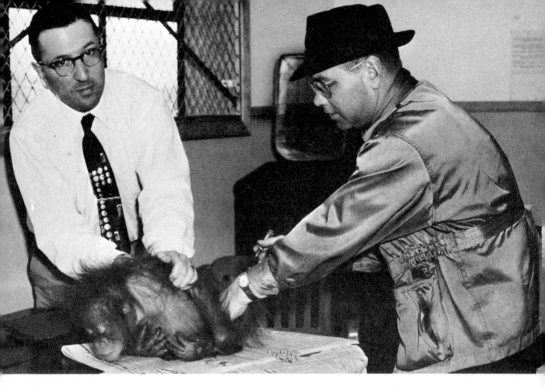

An Orangutan gets an injection.

TLC In Captivity

A six-month-old female Asiatic Elephant gets a bottle.

Cape Buffalo enjoy refreshment.

The broken horn of a female Sable Antelope is corrected at the Overton Park Zoo, Memphis. (*by R.H. Mattlin*)

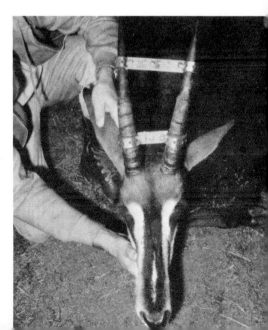

to do a book about your business!" And without hesitation I replied, "It's a good idea. How much will it cost me?"

To my amazement he assured me the book would cost me nothing, that if my story were interesting enough we would get an advance from a legitimate trade publisher. To this I jumped up, slammed the desk, and shouted, "Never in my life has a crazy man come into my office to tell me he can get me money for being me!" But then I hastily added, "What do I do?"

He instructed me to dictate my life and my business story into a tape recorder and send him the reels.

Never let it be thought Zeehandelaar goes into a partnership— even in writing a book—without caution. So I questioned this aggressive intruder as to what books he had previously written and told him that—regardless of what he said—before I could even entertain such a far-fetched idea as doing a book I would first consult my lawyer.

In a matter-of-fact fashion, Paul Sarnoff listed the books he had published and told me to call my lawyer immediately—which I did. After being assured I would be fully protected every step of the way I shook hands with Sarnoff—and the deal was done.

The whole thing took twenty minutes. But after Sarnoff had gone I sat as if in half-a-dream. Suddenly I realized I had reached the ripe old age of fifty and fate was handing me a chance to stop and look back.

I remember accepting an order from a zoo in the West for a pair of baby gorillas: one male, and one female. Understandably, the sex of wild baby gorillas is rather difficult to determine— especially when doting mother gorillas invariably loom nearby. But I took the order anyway, and let it out to a licensed big game hunter in Africa— with the proviso that he ship the pair together, as specified in the zoo's order.

The hunter—who considered this an idiotic order—completely disregarded my instructions and promptly shipped me a male. According to the terms of the zoo's order I could not make

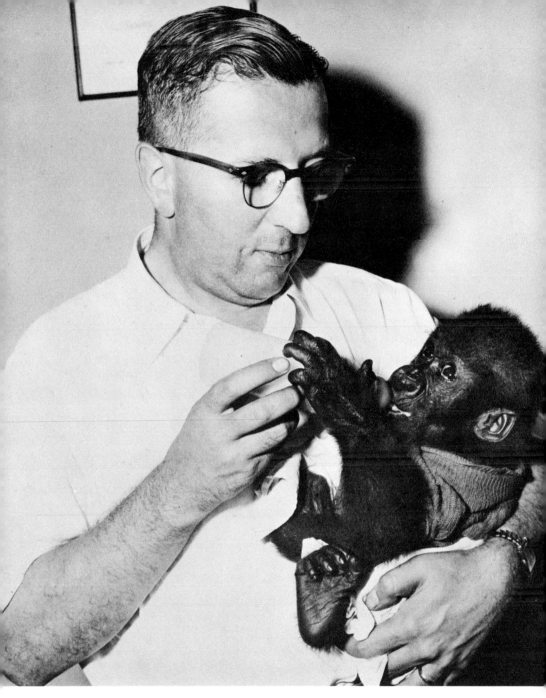

Baby Lowland Gorilla is nursed by F.J. Zeehandelaar.

delivery of a single animal and was faced with the problem of caring for a six-month-old baby gorilla until a female showed up from the same source. Since the animal had a value of about $5,000 I hated the idea of entrusting it to a dog kennel or zoo. Instead, and after a good deal of debate, I persuaded my good wife to make this baby gorilla part and parcel of the Zeehandelaar ménage. Because my wife already had had some firsthand experience with human babies, she looked after the gorilla as if it were another little Zeehandelaar.

For three weeks the baby gorilla romped about our house wearing diapers. He was regularly examined by the family pediatrician. And I still vividly remember this playful ape as he hopped up-and-down, watching TV with my two boys. Mercifully —and about two days before Christmas in the year of my gorilla-boarding-house-days—the female baby gorilla arrived safely at Idlewild and I completed the zoo's order for a pair of baby gorillas, as specified. I don't really know what would have happened if I had been forced to board the male gorilla for another six months.

On another occasion a western zoo sent me an order for a pair of zebras. The order specified that these animals be completely dewormed (rid of parasites) before shipping to the zoo. Zebras entering the United States are automatically quarantined before being delivered to any buyer. And at the quarantine station in Clifton, New Jersey, the animals are not only examined, but are also treated to rid them of ticks, excess parasites (nematodes), etc. Therefore, the zoo director's directive that his beasts be dewormed was obviously extraneous. As every naturalist knows, a certain amount of nematodes are not unusual in any healthy zebra. So it was quite natural for the zebras in question to contain a minimum number of nematodes in their intestines when they were trucked from Clifton to the western zoo.

About a month after this delivery, a package looking like a shoebox (wrapped in brown paper, and with tiny pinholes in its top), arrived in the mail. My suspicions aroused, I gingerly unwrapped and opened the box—all the while careful not to spill out its contents. Under the cover of the box was a letter from the western zoo director which read:

> Dear Zeehandelaar:
>
> Some months ago I ordered two zebras without worms.
> They arrived with worms.
> Here are the worms. . . .

The box, of course, was literally alive with crawling, wriggling parasites. If the box had broken in transit, and the nematodes had been accidentally freed from the box during its mailing, these parasites could have infected the water supply, or other animals, or even humans. When I talk about the reckless stupidity of a learned person like this zoo director doing such a dangerous thing as mailing a box full of wriggling nematodes, I'm usually asked, "What did *you* do with them?" And I promptly answer, "What do you think I did? I mailed them back."

Very often I receive friendly advice from people who themselves seek to profit from this advice. One day in 1960, a travel agency operator collared me and convinced me it would make sense (since I already had so many contacts with white hunters) to arrange for African safaris. And the travel agent told me I would receive 15 percent of the gross charges, because of allowances from the airlines, the hotels, and the white hunters.

Aided by friendly publicity in the local press, the idea caught fire more quickly than I could ever have imagined. I was literally overwhelmed with requests from jaded people seeking adventure in Hemingwayland. It seemed at last I had hit upon a simple, easy-to-arrange business to keep Zeehandelaar running the animal importing business and running to the bank. Little did I know what I was letting myself in for.

The customers who actually made safaris via my reservations filed an enormous number of complaints. They did not find the animals they had wanted as trophies; they could not get licenses; they ran into bad weather; they did not get good guides, etc., etc. Here I was minding my animal business some 6,000 miles away from safari country—with no logical way to sensibly take care of customers' complaints except by refunding money. The Zeehandelaar safari tours quickly followed the dodo bird into extinction.

A well-meaning friend came up with the idea that it might be more profitable to rent animals than to arrange for their import and sale. I decided to give this scheme a try.

A department store in Boston needed a certain kind of elephant for a promotion stunt and planned to display the beast in its window during a certain week of the year. The price they were willing to pay for the week's rental made it worthwhile to import an Indian elephant for the purpose. Naturally, once the beast was used for the display it would be returned to me and I could either sell it or rent it elsewhere. The idea was quite appealing. So I blithely entered into a contract to deliver the animal on the week scheduled—allowing much more than enough time for the elephant's travels from India to Boston by boat.

Less than a week before the ship bearing my rental cargo was due to arrive in Boston, its propeller shattered after striking an unidentified object in the Atlantic near Bermuda. The stricken ship limped into Hamilton for emergency repairs.

A week passed, and the ship made no progress at all in the repairs department. Meanwhile, the elephant was eating hay contentedly as I worried about meeting my deadline in Boston— a deadline approaching with alarming speed.

What was I to do? Normally, when ships become immobilized one can always depend on Pan American Airways. So I flew to Bermuda and arranged to have the elephant flown via Pan Am to Boston in sufficient time to meet the department store's deadline. But it seems that elephants, like camels and mules, have minds of their own. This pesky pachyderm didn't protest as she

Baby Indian Elephant put ashore in Bermuda.

was hauled up out of the ship's hold, swung through the air via a cargo sling, and landed on the quay. But no amount of cajoling, coaxing, goading, or blustering could move this animal up the narrow gangplank leading into the plane. In fact, neither bananas in the front nor pressure in the rear could make this monster walk the plank. As a result my elephant was marooned in Bermuda for weeks.

In the meantime the rental date had arrived—and gone. So too vanished my profit. And even after I managed to rid myself of the marooned elephant, the expense of maintaining her during the unexpected delay in transit caused considerable pain in my bank account.

Gradually it dawned upon me that diversification was not the proper path to profits in the wild animal business. I decided that the name of the game for me had to be "concentration." And so I abandoned every other kind of money-making idea and concentrated thereafter on the animal supply business.

Looking back, it wasn't easy to become successful in this business. In the early days I was asked by zoo directors to quote prices on animals I had never heard of! But in each case I dutifully copied down the genus and told the interested parties I'd let them know.

During this time I initiated a frenetic effort in self-education by rapidly collecting animal books and zoological texts. By dipping regularly into these books—some in English, as well as German, French and Dutch—I managed to acquire a smattering of expertise in wild animal taxonomy. Then I decided I would concentrate on supplying buyers with animals that were almost universally desired, but difficult to obtain. Eventually I began getting bids instead of constant requests for quotations. In other words—and just like in any other business where the price is made by the party most anxious for action—armed with *firm* bids I now could make effective delivery arrangements, knowing, with all factors normal, I could come out with profit. As is so often the case, however, profit can turn out to be quite illusory when things go wrong.

Since the success of my business basically depends upon the actions and the compliance of both animals and human beings, the failures that can arise are seldom attributed to the teletype machines, or to errors in paperwork. Indeed, important to every animal shipment to America—in addition to the buyer, the dealer, the regulatory agencies, and the shipper—are the suppliers, and, of course, the animals themselves.

And most wild animal supply begins with the hunters.

Pair of Snow Leopards (*Cheyenne Mountain Zoo, Colorado Springs*)

White-tailed Gnu (*The New York Times*)

Giant Red Kangaroo (*Los Angeles Zoo*)

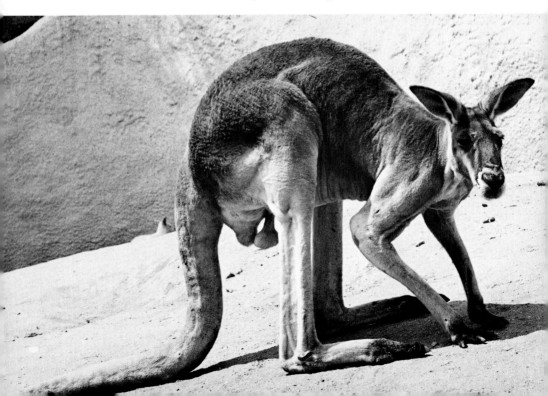

Oryx Beisa (*San Diego Zoo*)

African Black Rhino (*Kurt Müller*)

Grevy Zebra

Mother and baby Baringo Giraffe (*by F.D. Schmidt, San Diego Zoo*)

African Black Rhino (*Cheyenne Mountain Zoo, Colorado Springs*)

Mother and baby Dromedary Camel (*Los Angeles Zoo*)

Hermann Ruhe, Jr., Director of Hanover Zoo, Germany (right) inspects home of a newly-born Asiatic Elephant.

Pair of White Rhino (*Overton Park Zoo, Memphis*)

Adersi Duiker

Giant Panda

Eland (*Los Angeles Zoo*)

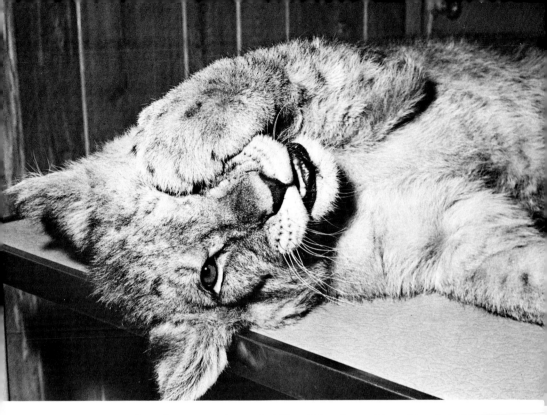

Backward running Lion Cub (*Macy Westchester Newspapers*)

Siberian Ibex

Burro (*Atlanta Zoo*)

Lake Baikal Seal

Lowland Nyala (*by Ron Garrison, San Diego Zoo*)

Wolverine (*Los Angeles Zoo*)

Bat-eared Fox (*Los Angeles Zoo*)

Family of Gelada Baboons

Okapi (*C. Richard Woodrum, San Francisco Zoo*)

5.
The Animal Hunters

There seem to be two distinctly divided classes of Americans: those who enjoy hunting, and those who hate it. To hunt, specifically to search out and kill one of the Lord's creatures, has always been anathema to me, as it is to those animal hunters who supply specimens for live exhibit at circuses, zoos, parks, and other nature spots. These often intrepid people are not interested in killing, or stuffing, or mounting their prey for display. Their skill in stalking and bringing wild animals to bay is used strictly to "bring them back alive." And to be good at their chosen trade, these hunters must be intensely interested in the well-being of the animals they capture.

These animal hunters—more appropriately labeled "animal trappers"—have a much tougher task than most people would imagine. First they must track down the wild animals they are after; then they must capture the beasts without injuring them. The specimens must then be brought safely to a collecting station, and suitably stored for future shipment. Eventually the animals are shipped from the collection station to buyers. The real trick, of course, is for the hunter to capture—and bring into the collection station—a healthy, undamaged animal.

Alas, this is often more easily said than done. Of course, with modern technology animal trappers can use anesthetic darts to bring down and immobilize even the most dangerous animal long enough to get it into a proper cage for transport. But it is believed that such a procedure often causes harmful effects to the captured animal. While adverse effects may not necessarily be evident as soon as the animal regains consciousness, serious injury, and even death, can follow after the animal is already on display.

Fortunately there are methods of capturing wild animals without first putting them to sleep. For example, zebras, wildebeeste (gnus), and giraffes can be captured in a humane fashion, using a jeep or scout car. The hunters rig the car with special poles protruding from the sides of the vehicle. The jeep takes off across the veldt in pursuit of a herd of zebras, and as the fast-moving car comes alongside one, one of the hunters uses the outstretched pole to lasso the running animal about the neck. The driver of the jeep regulates his speed so that the animal is not injured as the vehicle brakes to a stop. Of course, this is not the approved cowboy style, but it is quite satisfactory in securing uninjured specimens.

Obviously not every wild beast can be successfully lassoed. To catch baby rhinos in India, the animal trappers dig and camouflage pits—deep enough to keep the intended victim prisoner, but not deep enough to injure it from the fall—and then chase their baby prey (no sane animal trapper would even think of stalking fully grown rhinos for shipment to a zoo) away from the mothers and along the path to the pit. Once a baby rhino drops into the pit, it can be easily roped and dragged into a transport cage.

Unfortunately not every animal can be trapped without damage or injury. In Siberia, where the snow leopards roam, the hunters who seek live specimens for display purposes cannot win their trophies without the use of animal traps. These are the steel traps so familiar to both moviegoers and devotees of Jack London's books. Invariably, when a luckless leopard is trapped, one of its paws is damaged. And because this magnificent animal is quite ferocious, it fights until it breaks one or two teeth in vain attempts to bite through the steel jaws of the trap.

In Tibet and Southern China the elusive giant panda can be taken captive only by a rope snare. The hunter must make sure that the noose not only slips over the panda's neck, but also over its front legs—otherwise the animal can choke to death while trying to break loose of the noose.

In my endeavor to effectively import animals from almost all parts of the world, I had to seek out and initiate business relations with leading hunters and suppliers in almost every country. To do this required a study in information retrieval which covered many years of work. Eventually I compiled a sort of world census involving leading wild animal trappers and collectors. As a constant part of my study I weeded out the unreliable animal trappers from the reliable ones.

Actually the number of reliable hunters in India, Africa, and Australia can be easily counted on both hands. My years of collecting the required data were not without great personal expense—and sometimes worry and anguish. Although I am naturally reluctant to reveal who the reliable trappers are, and what supply sources I use, I have no such reluctance in exposing the deeds if not always the true names of some of the unreliable sources I have encountered during my career.

Many years ago—and long before I knew better—I came in contact with an Italian hunter named Antonio Lido. This man, a first-class crook, came to see me bearing a beautiful book filled with glassine envelopes which displayed color photos of some of the world's rarest animals, such as the dibatag, the mountain nyala, etc. The habitat of these animals (there are virtually none in captivity) is Ethiopia. Lido made a great display of his Ethiopian hunting licenses and letters of recommendation from Ethiopian officials—as he assured me he could deliver any Ethiopian animals I wanted to order. He also offered to act as my exclusive agent in Ethiopia, provided I gave him a small deposit ($750). Blindly trusting this swindler, I handed him the $750 —and he promptly disappeared.

Years later I found he had pulled similar swindles on well-known American zoos, extracting as much as $3,000 a zoo on the promise that he would act as their "exclusive" agent in Ethiopia and ship them the rare animals they so avidly sought. Not so oddly, while Lido was working the field in America, his lovely wife was trying the same kind of swindles in South America. But I never learned whether she was as successful as her persuasive husband.

Shortly after being gulled by Lido I heard of another hunter who reputedly had access to rare animals. His last name was Crochetti (I never learned his first name) and his base of operations was Fort-Lamy, Chad. Crochetti supposedly had a prime source of rare Sahara antelopes and I naturally wanted to be in on such a source. But having been burned by Lido, I approached Mr. Crochetti in a very different manner.

As a favor to me a friend of mine went from Germany to look up Crochetti on his home base. My friend found that this so-called "source" made a habit of collecting advances from animal fanciers and zoos, and invariably failed to deliver the goods. In fact, over an ice-cold beer in Fort-Lamy, Crochetti was insensitive enough to complain to my friend, "I am out of money. Those bloody Americans don't send any more funds." On the basis of my friend's report I joined the "bloody" Americans—and sent Crochetti nothing. Perhaps I did lose a potential source of animal supply, but I assuredly prevented a tax loss on that year's return, a loss I could easily have had by paying Crochetti a cash advance.

In the olden—and perhaps not so golden—days of the wild animal business, specimens arrived in American and Continental zoos via two major methods: (1) an expedition was financed and sent to a specific area to bring back as many live specimens of all kinds of birds and animals possible, and (2) certain flamboyant animal trappers would collect a shipload of many species of birds, reptiles, and mammals and sail the ship into a European or American port, hoping to dispose of the cargo at a profit.

Many books have been written about special expeditions and safaris in the search of specific wild animals. But not too many books have been written about those great "collectors" who loaded up a ship in Africa or India and sailed it into the Mediterranean, where avid buyers flocked around them to compete for the ship's cargo. Such a book, if it were ever written—that is if the truth could somehow be separated from the apocrypha— would necessarily concern a remarkable character named Lothar Behrend.

Behrend, before World War II, was accustomed to collecting a great cargo of exotic and other birds and animals. He would then wire the largest wild animal buyers and fanciers in Europe saying he would arrive, in Marseilles, for example, aboard the SS *U-NAME-IT* on such-and-such a day. But because of World War II, currency restrictions, conservation laws, and import and export regulations to and from various countries, Lothar Behrend (fat and past middle-age) found himself literally penniless in Buenos Aires. He had reached the nadir of his career and it looked like he was finished. But just as all hope seemed lost, he met a young Swiss trying to peddle DDT for Geigy Chemicals in South America and entered into a partnership with him.

By supplying capital, and by being willing to take Behrend's orders, Peter Ryhiner (the Swiss) found himself at the field end of a bizarre wild animal partnership never duplicated before or after. After an apprenticeship involving cleaning animal cages, Ryhiner went out on safari to trap animals and birds, while Behrend remained in Buenos Aires, disposing of the birds and beasts via cable and radiogram to buyers all over the world.

Behrend, of course, was an innovative person when it came to getting orders and effecting delivery. Once, for example, he received an order from Zürich for a shipment of skunks. Since it was a rush order, Behrend decided to fly the animals to Switzerland. But no airline in its right mind would undertake hauling a crate full of nondeodorized skunks while carrying passengers. So Behrend had the box labeled "FINCHES. VERY DELICATE." And the crate was placed aboard an overseas plane. The plane got as far as Rio de Janeiro before a steward accidentally kicked the crate. Thereupon the plane made a hurried landing.

When it came to juggling payments and finances, Behrend proved again to be a clever master. Peter Ryhiner became an apt pupil of his partner in the process. His adventures and misadventures with Lothar Behrend are delightfully chronicled in *The Wildest Game* by Ryhiner and Mannix (London: Cassell, 1959).*

My first contact with Peter Ryhiner is erroneously detailed in this entertaining book. I quote from the book: "As the ship approached the dock a Cadillac half-a-block long and covered with gleaming chrome came tearing up and stopped with a scream of brakes. Two men jumped out and ran to the edge of the dock. One of them shouted, 'Is Peter Ryhiner the animal catcher on board?' "

The car was not a Cadillac; I drive a Pontiac station wagon. Moreover, Ryhiner had sent me an SOS to come to Boston because he was stranded with a cargo of valuable wild animals and found himself unable to pay the charges for freight, etc. My first question was, "How much money do you need?"

In any event, that is how I first came in contact with this gregarious Swiss, who calls himself an "animal catcher." Today he is in Switzerland renting storks to wedding parties (a good-luck thing the Swiss indulge in) instead of on safari in Africa or Asia.

Probably the most famous of the so-called animal trappers with whom I came into business contact is Heini Demmer. This Austrian entrepreneur inveigled the Chinese Communists into letting go of Chi-Chi, a giant panda—certainly a rare specimen—

---

* Published in U.S.A. by J. B. Lippincott, Philidelphia.

by promoting a swap deal involving some $7,000 in animals. At the time, this animal was worth at least $25,000. But instead of immediately reselling this rare specimen, Demmer decided to make some more money by displaying the panda in various places —for a fee. It has been reported that Demmer cleaned up at the rate of $1,000 a week (plus such extras as free hotel rooms and laundry for both him and his wife) by showing the panda in several European zoos. He even managed somehow to extract this fee from the East Berlin zoo!

In early September 1958 Chi-Chi arrived in London, where she is now a resident of the London Zoo. The authorities there paid her master the usual rental fee plus amenities. But the animal aroused such interest that the zoo bought the beast for 10,000 pounds sterling (at that time, $28,000). So far there have been two vain attempts to mate Chi-Chi—the only live giant panda on display outside the Communist world—with the Soviet giant panda, An-An.

Until now I have spoken only of my encounters with male animal trappers. It would be a crass insult to the fair sex if, in a discussion of the trade, I neglected to mention the ladies employed in that uncertain business.

Believe it or not there are a number of female animal trappers scattered all over the world. But the only lady animal hunter I ever dealt with was Diana Hartley of Rumuruti, Kenya. This remarkable lady had an uncanny way with animals—almost as if she could speak their language. I vividly remember the time she escorted a shipment of giraffes from Mombasa to New York. Shortly after the ship docked she held a press conference. Among the many members of the fourth estate was a bat-eared fox. Watching newsmen quaff champagne is not a new experience for me; but watching Diana's pet bat-eared fox daintily lap up champagne from a crystal glass was almost more than a teetotaler like me could stand!

Diana, a fiercely independent female, was related to the famous hunter, Carr Hartley—with whom I still do business. Regrettably

I was compelled to stop doing business with Diana. She had a penchant for raising and training lion cubs, but one day one of her maturing students suddenly attacked—and clawed her to death.

One lady animal hunter lived in Pittsburgh—but her operations base was in South America, particularly along the Amazon River. She specialized in small mammals, snakes, and exotic birds. This woman had a great gimmick: In order to attract attention at the annual conventions of the American Association of Zoological Parks & Aquariums (hereinafter AAZPA) she usually wore a unique hat. Atop her fancy bit of millinery was a very large cage —containing a number of colorful birds busily flitting and flying.

Another woman associated with the wild animal business is Peter Ryhiner's wife, Mercia, a beautiful Eurasian who was once an airline-ticket clerk in Singapore, and later became an integral part of her husband's hunting team. She soon became adept with the big cats, and naturally, she learned to raise the baby leopards, tigers, lions, etc. on bottled milk. On one occasion she lost a piece of her posterior when one of the cats decided to vary its diet.

I have never felt the need to make a more thorough study of the female angle of the wild animal trapping and hunting business, but because women have permeated almost every other profession in their quest for equality with men, chances are there are more women in the wild animal business today than there used to be.

Whether the animal hunter is male or female does not really matter: Very few animals, if any at all, would ever be captured without the indispensable aid of natives. Let us examine, for example, the time-honored method of catching Indian tigers.

Most people already know that the movie version is to dig a huge pit across a forest trail, camouflage the mouth of the pit with a leafy cover, and tie the traditional buffalo calf or sacrificial goat near the covered opening as bait.

The real-life method is quite different—and it requires the aid of many natives. The natives dig a pit twenty-four feet deep and about fifteen feet square. Then they stake a buffalo calf inside the pit itself, and construct a stockade fence about six feet high around the perimeter of the pit.

The tiger, lured by the calf, jumps over the stockade, lands in the pit, and devours the animal. Then a cover resting on the stockade is built over the entire pit, and a hole is left in the middle of this roof. Meanwhile a door is cut in the side of the stockade just large enough to accommodate the door of the transport cage. This cage door slides open and is kept raised to permit the mouth of the cage to remain open. A small hole about a foot square is cut in the rear of the transport cage directly opposite the sliding door.

To eventually lead the tiger up to the mouth of the transport cage, several natives first bring baskets of dirt and dump it down into the pit itself. The tiger gradually rises toward the roof of his prison and begins to leap and hurl his body at the roof in vain attempts to free himself. To quiet the raging beast the natives drop a few dead goats through the hole. Setting his rage aside, the tiger eats until he is sated—and is sluggish for some time thereafter.

When the tiger rises to the level of the mouth of the transport cage, the big question is how to get him into the cage itself. The Indians have solved this problem by using trained dogs, about the size of a fox. The natives, as soon as they think it's safe, drop one of these fox-like dogs into the pit. In no time at all, the tiger goes for the dog, but this agile little animal dashes into the transport cage and darts out the hole in its rear. The tiger, blindly pursuing the little dog, rushes into the transport cage—and the native holding the cage door drops it home! A bystander, once exclaimed, "I wouldn't have that little dog's job for all the gold in Mysore."

With the advance of modern technology, it isn't too farfetched to envision an eventual computerized capture of wild animals, but it is rather difficult to imagine the trapping of a young male tiger, full of fight, by using a desktop computer linked to a time-sharing system connected to the telephone. It is really quite difficult to

foresee—even beyond the year 2000—the trapping of wild
animals without the help of good-natured natives.

It has already been pointed out that animals trapped for
exhibits abroad are generally not endangered during capture. But
I must emphasize that they do undergo a series of trials and
tribulations in transit, which could kill them long before they
arrive at their destinations. In the jungle, of course, the zebra is
imperiled by the lion. The lion in turn is imperiled by packs of
hyenas. This is nature's way; and it has been so since the
beginning of time. But the greatest danger to animals caught for
display purposes does not arise from the natural ecosystem. It stems
mainly from humans. And this danger begins precisely at the
moment the hunters place the animals in transport cages for the
trip to the collecting stations.

6.
The Animal Shippers

Wild animal collecting stations, scattered in various parts of the world, are essential to the wild animal business. They not only facilitate the accumulation of large animal cargoes, but also aid the importer in complying with certain regulations of the United States Department of Agriculture.

Long ago the Agriculture Department ruled that before wild ruminants, such as giraffes, antelopes, etc., could be brought into the United States they must be held for a period of at least sixty days at a selected foreign quarantine station. There are approved stations in such locations as Hamburg, Germany; Naples, Italy; Mombasa, Kenya; etc. A typical station of this type is the one currently operated by the great European firm of wild animal dealers, L. Ruhe.

The Ruhe concern has been internationally famous for more then one hundred years. Basically it services European zoos, while I basically service American and Canadian zoos. This very fine firm possesses the only indoor animal compound in the world, at a place some twenty-five miles south of Hannover. By virtue of a very friendly arrangement, I have for many years cooperated with this concern—and we have helped each other in the process.

Reticulated Giraffes in "stopover" at Mombasa Quarantine station . . .

The Grand Tour for Animals

. . . and upon arrival in New York.

Scandinavian Reindeer meets "reception committee" after transatlantic voyage.

At times I send large shipments to Ruhe at the Hannover Zoo to be held for later transport to my customers in North America. Even though the animals are my property and risk, the Ruhe people have always looked after my living merchandise as if it were their own. Because about 70 percent of my business has at one time or another been held at Hannover, I regard that office as if it were my own. A telex machine in my New Rochelle office is directly connected to a mate in the Ruhe office in Germany. And when the signal bell sounds either in New Rochelle or in Hannover we jump to the machine, because it is clacking away about the wild animal business.

Naturally my office also receives telex messages from other collecting stations and holding stations. These messages may eventually mean profit or loss, aggravation or pleasure, or any combination of extremes.

On the morning of March 8, 1968 one of my machines began clacking an urgent message from an enterprising animal collector in Holland (Code name "Jacob"). His wire began:

> JUST BOT TEN HOODED CRANES L75E FOB CHINA.
> SOLD SO FAR TO USA (PRIVATE CLIENT NO
> ZOO) ONE PR DLRS 1250 PR . . . PAYMENT ADVANCED.
>
> HAVE YOU CLIENTS, FUNDS FOR JOINTS, ANY PROSPECTS?
> (PLEASE DON'T ASK WHO IS SO STUPID TO BUY TEN
> HOODED CRANES BECAUSE YOU KNOW THE REPLY.
> THAT IS ME.)

Jacob thus told me he had bought ten Chinese hooded cranes for a gross cost (before freight, etc.) of $1,800; had sold off one pair to a private American bird fancier for $1,250; and offered me the following alternatives: I could offer the birds as an agent to my clients, or I could go "partners" with him and split the profits— if I put up half the costs. His parenthetical remark about being "stupid" was quite apropos; because at that time Americans were forbidden to buy any animals from the Chinese Communists, so how could I have obtained the necessary permits to import his cranes into the United States? In any event—and to retain his goodwill—I immediately wired back:

COMPETITION HERE $1650 PR CIF JFK. DONT
MENTION CHINA. PROSPECTS YES. JOINT NO.
WHAT IS YR REAL COST 1/1 CIFHD?

My wire told Jacob the current going price for a pair of similar birds, including (CIF) the cost of insurance and freight to Kennedy International Airport. I declined to go joint venture with him on such a deal; but to keep him interested I asked him what his real cost of a pair (1/1) of cranes (one male and one female) would be, delivered in Holland. In this manner I politely rebuffed a Continental entrepreneur who apparently considered Communist China to be as friendly to him as the United States—if it provided him the means to make profit.

Making a profit in my business isn't always my primary consideration. Accommodation of my customers, however, is. But the confusion of existing Government agency regulations makes customer accommodation increasingly difficult. The importer must know which department handles which animals, and how many agencies are actually involved. For example: The Agriculture Department has complete jurisdiction over the importation of animals and birds subject to diseases—possibly carriers of diseases —harmful to other animals. And the Department of Health, Education and Welfare regulates the entrance into this country of animals such as primates and psittacine birds (parrots, etc.) which may carry diseases contagious to humans. The regulations are so confusing that most sophisticated zoo people are convinced that primates come under the jurisdiction of the Agriculture Department rather than HEW. To make matters even more complex and burdensome for the importer, most animals entering the United States often fall into the regulations of more than one agency, such as the Interior Department (Fish and Wild Life Service) and the Customs Bureau of the Treasury Department.

Because animal imports are almost drowned in a sea of red tape it has become increasingly popular for American zoos and American animal fanciers to try to buy wild animals born in captivity within the borders of the United States. This does not imply that by buying animals here the purchasers pay less than if the beasts were imported. Typical of such a case is the pair of giraffes, born at zoos in Texas and Tennessee, which I sold to the Abilene Zoo for $10,000. The reticulated male giraffe was born in Memphis in August 1968 and the female in November, in Dallas. I had originally arranged for a female born in the Detroit Zoo (same age as the male, born in August 1968) to accompany the male giraffe, but the Detroit female expired before she could be shipped—and so we all had to wait for the Dallas specimen to grow old enough to make the shipment.

The shipping of such animals from one point to another requires much more than a modicum of planning and care. The animals must be so placed inside a truck that they can be comfortable in their cramped quarters, that they can be easily fed, and that their quarters can be kept relatively clean. To handle this matter I almost always employ the services of Harry Overbaugh, who I feel is probably the most qualified person in the country to haul and deliver giraffes and antelopes. Often I am forced to secure his services more than a year in advance—and in the case of contemplated zoo swappings, even before the actual animals are born.

However, only approximate arrangements can be made for the services of such a trucker. The exact delivery date and the precise hour are often difficult, if not impossible, to meet. And so I have developed the Zeehandelaar philosophy: "Dates and animals do not go together." Things go wrong, animals get ill, the truck breaks down—and more, much more. I was fortunate—I managed to move the aforementioned giraffes from Memphis and Dallas to their new home in Abilene, Texas without incident.

But I clearly recall a case where giraffes were being transported by ship from Mombasa to New York and the wrong kind

of fodder was loaded aboard. As the ship stood out to sea
for the month-long voyage to America, the giraffes
ate the poisonous fodder causing the skin on their faces
and heads to itch terribly. As a result they rubbed their heads
against the sides of their wooden crates with such force that the
skin was literally flayed off their faces, and they died at sea.
Through negligence this one error in the selection of fodder for
animals in transport caused an insurance claim of more than
$50,000. This, of course, was *not* one of my importations.

On October 12, 1968, it was my privilege and pleasure to
address a meeting of the Exotic Wildlife Association in Laredo,
Texas. This organization, made up of members from both public
and private wild animal zoos, compounds, and game preserves, was
formed with the primary purpose of preserving, exchanging, or
selling the excess animals born in their respective institutions.
Most of the members of the association are not USDA approved
and consequently they can purchase exotic wild ruminants only if
those animals were born in the United States. Nearly always the
source of such animals is a USDA approved zoo which predictably
charges what the traffic will bear. Yet the "nonapproved" buyer is
not entirely disadvantaged since the price he pays is usually not
greater than he would expect to pay for an imported wild
ruminant.

To understand this correctly, it is fitting to trace the voyage of
a single giraffe from the jungle to an American zoo through my
firm—and with the blessings of various agencies, especially the
USDA.

My bare cost to deliver such a specimen to a collecting
station at Arusha (Tanzania) would be about $1000. The animal
then has to be suitably crated, trucked, fed, and cleaned while
transported from Arusha to Mombasa—at an approximate cost of
$300. The animal has to be insured from the moment it arrives
at the collecting station until it is ultimately delivered to its
American purchaser. This would cost approximately $1,800. In
Mombasa the animal would have to be held for the required
USDA sixty-day stay at the approved foreign holding point. This

sojourn—if all went well and no veterinarian were needed to look after the sensitive beast—would cost approximately $600. At last the cud-chewing attraction reaches the port of New York safely (ocean freight $700) and is trucked away to Clifton to be quarantined for thirty days at an antiquated USDA facility. This stay costs $10 a day, or $300. Meanwhile, I would incur a financing expense of approximately $200 covering this shipment. To handle my annual volume with my own funds, I would need the resources of the old lady of Threadneedle Street. From Clifton there are additional trucking charges for the giraffe's trip to its ultimate American destination. Tabulating all these expenses, the actual cost would come to:

Cost in jungle	$1,000
Crating and transport to Mombasa	300
Insurance	1,800
60-day stay at Mombasa	600
Ocean freight	700
30-day Clifton quarantine	300
Financing expense	200
Local American trucking charges	200
Total	$5,100

Had the Abilene Zoo imported a pair of giraffes, the cost obviously would have exceeded $5,100 per animal—for in the above table I have not included a single cent of profit for Zeehandelaar. And to pervent Samuel Johnson's "No man but a blockhead ever wrote except for money," my principle is "Only a dummkopf imports wild animals for nothing." Moreover, had this zoo ordered their pair of giraffes as wild specimens (rather than offspring of animals born in American zoos) the institution would have had to wait six-to-eight months before even expecting delivery.

Notice that an expense of more than $1,000 is created by the quarantine regulations of the Agriculture Department in the importation of a giraffe. And it should also be remembered that the USDA permits the importation of wild ruminants only to *approved* American zoos.

The following excerpt from USDA regulations sets forth the standards for approval:

> Approval of a zoological park for the receipt and maintenance of imported animals . . . shall be on the basis of an inspection, by an authorized representative of the Department [of Agriculture], of the physical facilities of the establishment and its methods of operation. Standards for acceptable physical facilities shall include satisfactory pens, cages or enclosures in which the animals can be maintained so as not to be in contact with the general public and free from contact with domestic livestock; natural or established drainage from the zoological park which will avoid contamination of land areas where domestic livestock are kept or with which domestic livestock may otherwise come in contact; provision for the disposition of manure, other wastes, and dead ruminants and swine within the zoological park; and other reasonable facilities considered necessary to prevent the dissemination of diseases from the zoological park. The operator of the zoological park shall have available the services of a full-time or part-time veterinarian, or a veterinarian on a retainer basis, who shall make periodic examinations of all animals maintained at the zoological park for evidence of disease; who shall make a post-mortem examination of each animal that dies; and who shall make a prompt report of suspected cases of contagious or communicable diseases to appropriate state or federal livestock sanitary officials.

But how do the nonapproved places sidestep the restrictions of a Federal agency? Basically the method involves arrangements between the approved zoos and the nonapproved buyers.

For example, if a certain nonapproved American game farm wants to buy a species of rare Ethiopian antelope, the owner of the farm makes arrangements with an approxed zoo to import several animals. He pays the zoo for the importation with a donation to the zoo. Thereupon the zoo orders the importation of the antelopes. When these animals bear offspring, the zoo makes a gift of the offspring to the donor. And since wild ruminants born in approved zoos do not fall under Agriculture Department restrictions, the approved zoos can release, peddle, or trade the offspring of such exotic animals to zoos or game preserves not approved by the USDA.

What I am trying to say is that more zoos and game farms should be put into approved classes. But reform in the wild

animal business is probably as slow to evolve as in any other area
of our bureaucracy-burdened country.

Speed, coordination, and communication are the backbone of
my business—but the ultimate success of an animal import
depends both on the people who help to dismantle the red-tape
curtain that hampers the movement of the animals, and also on
(1) the manner in which the animal is boxed or crated, (2) the
care given it in transit, and (3) the environmental conditions it
encounters along the way.

For example, last year an importation of mine, consisting of two
polar bears, six colobi (African monkeys), and twelve penguins,
was brought into Kennedy International Airport by Lufthansa for
transfer to American carriers—and thence to zoos in the South
and the West. My coauthor, who had never before seen wild
animals in the shipping stage, met me at the airport, where I
introduced him to the man I believe to be one of the most
gifted customs brokers in the business, Joe Santarelli. It was about
9:00 A.M. when we met. The planes on which these animals were
scheduled to leave JFK were to depart between 1:00 and 2:00
P.M. In the meantime Joe would first have to clear all the papers
with customs, and the various agencies involved, and then see to
it that the animals were hauled safely from Lufthansa to the
airlines taking them to their final destination. He would also see
to it that the animals were actually loaded aboard the correct
carrier.

While Joe rushed off to take care of these matters, Sarnoff and
I went over to Lufthansa to inspect the incoming shipment. The
first question my overstuffed coauthor asked was, "Isn't it cruel to
confine the polar bears in such small crates—with only one
opening covered by a rusty grill?"

His question was not surprising. I patiently explained that if
the container were larger, the bear would be able to crouch in a
corner of the crate, summon its strength, and launch itself in fury
at the opening. Chances are the bear would then break out of the

crate and escape. But by designing the wooden box so there is
not enough room for the bear to assault the opening of his
temporary prison, the animal is kept enclosed for transport—and
is also prevented from possible injury.

As an interesting sidelight to the shipping procedures, we were
able to witness the difference in character of caged animals—as
dramatically illustrated by these bears. One animal evidently had
become resigned to captivity and remained docile and quiet. He
actually seemed to relax while awaiting transfer to the American
carrier. But the other animal angrily resented its captivity. It kept
snarling and growling and trying vainly to bite through the steel
wire covering the front of its crate.

Meanwhile the penguins (six to a crate) seemed in good
condition. Their crates were divided by plywood walls into six
compartments housing the penguins in a vertical position. The
tops of these crates were covered with wire mesh so that light and
air could enter the penguins' area, but they couldn't possibly hop
out. The colobi's crates also were ingeniously designed to give the
animals plenty of room to move about, but the boxes were strong
enough to fend off attacks if the animals had tried to escape. Here
too the differences in individual animals were dramatically
illustrated. Some of the creatures were docile and seemingly
content, while others kept raging and launching their bodies
forcibly against the wire-mesh-covered face of their temporary
cages.

As another example of the importance of the actual crating
methods. I cite the manner in which zebras are crated. When they
are shipped to the United States on cargo ships, zebras require
special crates just cramped enough to prevent the animals from
breaking their legs while trying to kick their way to freedom. The
sides of a zebra crate rise to about the point in the zebra's neck
that meets its shoulders. And all during the voyage, the zebra's
neck remains free and unhampered in any way. Along the front
and rear sides of the crate—and running along the bottom of the
crate—are slot-like openings to facilitate flushing and cleaning.

Because zebras contain nematodes they can infect themselves from their own feces, and therefore must constantly be kept externally clean. This is a perfect illustration of the diligent care required for animals in transit.

The environmental temperature during transit is also an important consideration when shipping and transporting animals. In December 1968 a shipment of assorted animals, including one okapi worth about $17,500, arrived at the docks in Brooklyn. Because of union regulations about unloading over the weekend, the beasts were confined to shipboard during a severe snowstorm. When they were unloaded and shipped off to Clifton for quarantining I noticed something wrong with the okapi, and I began to worry.

My fears were confirmed when the okapi died "of a heart attack" while being inserted into the "squeeze box" for a blood test at the quarantine station. A few days later I visited this facility with my coauthor and as we were being escorted about the outmoded place I noticed one of the giraffes in this same shipment was sick.

"How do you know this?" Sarnoff asked. And I answered, "Look. Watch how this giraffe is chewing. You see his jaws are moving straight up and down and not grinding from side to side. Also, he does not ruminate 30 times per minute. This means he is sick."

Sure enough the veterinarian, Dr. Paul Lanphear, confirmed my diagnosis, and by swift action saved the valuable animal.

Amazing as it may seem, most people involved in the shipping and the forwarding of animals have a great deal of empathy, if not sympathy, for the caged creatures. I clearly remember a shipment of penguins that landed at Kennedy International Airport on a hot summer day and somehow missed the connecting carrier. As a result there was an interval of about six hours during which these Antarctic denizens were exposed to the peculiarly pressing heat that shimmers up from both runways and buildings in the Jamaica (Queens) meadows. Some kind employees of

F.J. Zeehandelaar and customs broker Joe Santarelli.

the cargo carriers managed to locate blocks of ice and some huge electric fans. They then set to and caused an artificially cool breeze to play over the penguins until the bizarre birds were sent to their air-conditioned plane.

In the not-so-rare event that animals shipped from overseas are grounded overnight at international airports, at least one facility in the U.S. has an animal hotel: that is the special ASPCA building at JFK. This "animalport" was officially opened by the ASPCA in 1957. Since then this facility has housed more than 600,000 animals, including cats, dogs, birds, and elephants. But by far the largest numbers of visitors have been soldiers' dogs, mascots of overseas men who preserve the free world. Fortunately the rates at this "animotel" are less than the Algonquin or the Waldorf. But the fact that such a facility even exists is comforting, to say the least.

Naturally I cannot always be on hand to watch incoming shipments or see that my animals enter and leave quarantine safely and arrive at their destination in good condition. That is why I thank the Lord for people like Joe Santarelli.

On March 25, 1969, I sent him the following letter:

Dear Joe:

Enclosed is the latest schedule of my travels. As you will note, starting this Sunday, March 30, I will be more or less away until May 9th—with interruption of a few days in the second and third week in April and approximately one week at the end of April.

To promote smooth operation, I submit a list of anticipated air shipments during that time, together with the names of suppliers, clients, prices, and 3321's.

I also submit the various scientific names and ask you to prepare the F&W forms if and when the shipments arrive, in case I am not available and have not done so myself.

I cannot, for obvious reasons, give you clearing and forwarding instructions (foreign and domestic) because flight schedules change from time to time.
We will have to play this by ear. . . .

The shipments involved tree kangaroos, clouded leopards, moustached monkeys, lesser pandas, capped langurs, gentoo penguins, sloth bears, polar bears, aardvarks, gibbons, and other animals. In all there were seven shipments while I was away, and Joe cleared and handled these shipments competently, effectively —and with a minimum of delay.

During the time Joe juggled my animal shipments I was quite busy traveling.

On April 1 and 2, 1969, I attended the Northeast Regional Zoo meeting in Rochester, New York, where among other activities I delivered a provocative presentation on zoo management to the assembled zoo people. On April 8 and 9, I appeared in a repeat performance before an audience at the Central USA Regional Zoo meeting in Kansas City. And on April 12, I flew to Amsterdam to participate in an AAZPA European Zoo Tour. On May 2, I returned home to face a barrage of protests from my coauthor concerning my delay in dictating this book onto the waiting tape-recorder reels.

7.
A Life in the Day of Z

Could Gogol possibly have had a wild animal dealer in mind when he wrote, "For the poor man the night is short?" By reverse reasoning for me, the day is long. Normally a typical day in my life begins with a phone call instead of an alarm clock. . . .

6:05 A.M.:   A Dallas zoo official phones me at home to complain that the plane bearing a leopard from me to his zoo has arrived at the Dallas Airport, but the leopard is missing.

6:10 A.M.:   Via phone, I awaken Joe Santarelli, my Kennedy cargo broker, and "politely" urge him to investigate the lost leopard at once. It takes me, of course, at least five minutes to get my message across, because of Santarelli's swearing (in more than one language).

6:20 A.M.:   Joe phones back and reports the Dallas-destined cat has been erroneously loaded on a San Francisco-bound plane.

6:22 A.M.:   I phone San Francisco and raise hell. Eventually an official promises to ship the wrong-way leopard back to Dallas as soon as possible.

6:25 A.M.:   Because of my wife's urging, I go back to bed.

7:25 A.M.:   An Air France phone call wakens me with the news of a chimpanzee arrival at Kennedy. Of the four apes in this shipment two are in good condition, one is under the weather, and one has died. The caller also volunteers that the consignee's name on the papers isn't quite clear. Then he asks if this shipment could be for me? I bark "NO" into the phone and hang up. Now I get out of bed to begin my business day, an hour and a half after it actually began.

8:00 A.M.:   Breakfast—with my wife, our two sons, and six cats.

8:25 A.M.:   I arrive at my New Rochelle office. If observing speed limits, official driving time is fifteen minutes from my house in Eastchester; but my normal driving time is nine minutes. My license was once suspended for traffic violations.

8:40 A.M.:   By this time I have already read the cables arriving from all parts of the world on my communications complex and have already replied where necessary. Naturally I yearn to attack the mail, but there is no mail.

8:50 A.M.:   I call the local postmaster to ask the daily question so many American businessmen have become accustomed to ask: "Where is my mail?" I get the usual answer.

F.J. Zeehandelaar at work in his office. (*Eric Zeehandelaar*)

9:00 A.M.: To my complete surprise, my mail arrives. But to my complete chagrin, my secretary doesn't. And things being so uptight in the secretarial sector it certainly isn't prudent for me to hand her an argument for coming in late. So I attack the mail myself and dictate the necessary replies into a tape recorder.

9:10 A.M.: Right in the middle of talking to myself a salesman for a foreign airline drops in to urge me to use the facilities of his airline, which I already use anyway.

9:11 A.M.: The airline salesman departs.

9:25 A.M.: My secretary arrives—smiling sweetly. I know between fussing over her desk and visiting the ladies' room it will take her a half-hour before she is ready for work—and by then it's almost time for the morning coffee break.

9:27 A.M.: A zoo director phones to tell me the cheetah I had delivered about ten days ago has died during the night. The director laments his zoo did not insure the cat. Sympathetically I murmur: "Too bad. But please mail me a check for the cheetah."

9:59 A.M.: My secretary heaves herself up to get coffee and asks me if I want mine light, as usual. By now I am on my second pack of Camels—without walking any miles.

10:20 A.M.: I call a steamship-lines official in New York City. It seems a scheduled shipment is due to arrive from Mombasa in a few days and the steamship people have no papers, no documents of any kind. Maybe the hunters left the papers in the jungle. Since there is no letter of credit involved I ask the official to please release the shipment. But he wants a guarantee from me that the nonexistent shipping papers are in order. This I refuse to do, because what if errors are made in the new papers and the old ones turn up? I instruct him to hold the animals on the pier until I straighten things out. He doesn't like this idea at all, but agrees to release the shipment somehow.

10:37 A.M.: My secretary is typing replies to my mail when the phone jangles again. This time a NASA official wants to know when the space agency can expect delivery of fifteen pigtail macaques ordered some time ago. I tell him the shipment hopefully should be in soon. Meanwhile I know these monkeys haven't even been caught yet.

10:48 A.M.: A Veterans Administration doctor in Ann Arbor, Michigan, phones to ask how soon he can receive six mature female rhesus monkeys. He requires that the monkeys be sexually mature, not too old, and with permanent dentition. I tell him "three weeks if the order is placed immediately." He says he'll let me know.

10:58 A.M.: A phone call from the quarantine station in Germany. Papers on a shipment from Chad announce the arrival of six male and three female addax. The papers sent to the quarantine station from my office describe a shipment of three male and six female antelopes of the same genus. What should they do? I ask them to change the papers to conform to the actual animals.

11:10 A.M.: A midwest zoo employee phones to announce his Mr. & Mrs. Zoo Director are arriving today on flight so-and-so and will be staying at Hotel So-and-So. What does he expect me to do? Come up with a pair of tickets for *Oh! Calcutta!*?

11:13 A.M. I call a local steakhouse to reserve a table for dinner for Mr. & Mrs. Zoo Director tomorrow night.

11:20 A.M. I start my third pack of Camels and wonder when I'll ever get the time to dictate my Zeebongo book. Suddenly my reverie is shattered when my secretary shoves a batch of unsigned letters under my Ben Franklin glasses.

NOON: Having signed all the letters, I down my fifth cup of coffee.

12:01 P.M.: Before I can get heartburn from the coffee I have to pick up the phone. It's the foreman at the

Clifton quarantine station with distressing news
that one of my oryxes is injured. While in its stall
at the station, this antelope somehow split one of
its horns; but the horn did not drop.

12:10 P.M.:   I contact my veterinarian and instruct him to drive
over to Clifton to look after the oryx's split horn.

12:30 P.M.:   Just as I am on the way out to lunch the telex
from Holland starts to clack. And the information
necessitates my sending out cables to many parts
of the world. Naturally I am anxious to receive the
answers, so I forget about eating. But I don't
forget about smoking. Since cigarettes may be
harmful to one's health, and since I am reluctant
to smoke too many Camels, I open a fresh box of
Dutch cigars.

2:00 P.M.:   A Walter Reed Hospital research bigwig phones
collect and talks for eighteen minutes. He doesn't
really know precisely what specifications are needed
for the animals his colleagues want to order. To
make matters worse, he can't even answer the
questions I ask.

2:22 P.M.:   Lufthansa phones announcing the anticipated arrival
of my shipment of shoebill storks at Kennedy, at
4 P.M. I decide to go to the airport to meet this
incoming shipment.

3:35 P.M.:   Having handled a host of miscellaneous details
cluttering up my desk I board my station wagon
for the trip to Kennedy.

4:00 P.M.:   By a minor miracle I arrive at the airport without
a speeding ticket. But concomitant with my coming

a dense fog settles over the field. I imagine I can
hear the Lufthansa plane circling overhead. But
if so it doesn't circle for long. The dispatcher tells
me matter-of-factly that due to the fog my shoebill
storks have flown north to Montreal.

4:15 P.M.:   A shipment of polar bear cubs arrives on KLM to
be transferred to TWA and flown to St. Louis on
the 7:30 P.M. passenger plane. The USDA
inspectors find the crates contain prohibited produce
and the crates are shunted over to the ASPCA
building for cleaning. By heroic efforts the crates
are released—after being cleaned—and the animals
are delivered to TWA for shipment.

7:00 P.M.:   I'm back in my office and the phone rings. It's a
TWA big-shot telling me the polar bears were
refused boarding permission because of the stench.

7:30 P.M.:   I locate Joe Santarelli bowling with his buddies in
a local alley. When his swearing dies down he
manages (by phone) to shift the smelly bears
from the TWA passenger plane to a TWA cargo
plane later that night.

7:45 P.M.:   Home for dinner.

8:55 P.M.:   I return to my office to take care of unfinished
cabling to Europe.

9:00 P.M.:   In the middle of telex-talking to Hannover, the
phone rings. A TWA employee claims one of the
polar bears is chewing its way through the grating
covering the crate. [Polar bears are very intelligent.
In July 1969, seven bears in the Chicago
Brookfield Zoo noticed a heavy rain had flooded

the moat surrounding their "island." The bears promptly swam ashore and headed directly for the snackbar. It seems they had been "casing" the refreshment stand for some time and eventually enjoyed the marshmallows most.]

9:05 P.M.:   Again I head for Kennedy. Now it's an emergency, so I drive faster than Zeehandelaar's normal speed. Again the Zeehandelaar luck holds. No ticket.

9:30 P.M.:   Ever try getting a carpenter at this time of night? Looking in the *Yellow Pages* doesn't help, either. Somehow I fix the cage before the polar bear breaks loose; and then I head back to my office.

11:00 P.M.:   Back at the office I arrange for tomorrow's work. Meanwhile I open my fourth pack of Camels. How long can anybody chew Dutch cigars?

MIDNIGHT: Local police, noticing the lights, come up to my office to check—and stay for free coffee. By the time they depart and I finish my work, it is past one o'clock in the morning.

1:30 A.M.:   I have just finished explaining to my patient wife the reasons I had to drive to Kennedy Airport and back twice in one day, when the phone rings. It's a St. Louis zoo official complaining the polar bears he expected on the 7:30 P.M. TWA passenger flight from Kennedy were not on the plane. I apologized for neglecting to wire that the bears were coming on the night TWA cargo plane. But I assure him if the TWA cargo plane didn't get

lost and wind up in Wichita, his zoo would get
the bears about 6:00 A.M. And wearily I hang up
—without remembering whether or not I had said
"good night."

From this sampling it can be readily understood that both my
life and my business involve communications. On more than one
occasion I have been called "communications crazy." In fact my
hobby is communications. And why not? Most of my business is
transacted by telephone, cable, telegraph, and telex. While I am
in the United States, I am *never* out of touch with my office.
Moreover, my secretary *always* knows where to reach me when
I am away from my office. Indeed, I carry an instrument in my
pocket which permits her to contact me at any time by sending
out a special signal or beep. For example if I am driving
somewhere and she wants to contact me she signals. On hearing
the beep, I immediately use the phone in my car to call my office.
(Normally, when accompanied by passengers unaware of this
arrangement, they jump as if shot when the beep blasts off. But
one day I was driving to Clifton to show the quarantine station to
my coauthor, and talking rapidly as the beep went off. "Did you
hear that?" I asked. And without blinking an eye he asked back
"Hear what?" And I said, "The beep signal." And he readily
admitted, "Oh that. I didn't have my hearing aid turned on.")

In order for me to exist as one of the world's busiest wild
animal dealers I must be turned on and tuned in almost eighteen
hours a day, seven days a week. It would, of course, help matters
if the people I deal with knew more about the animal specimens
they buy or sell. Strangely enough, about 90 percent of the people
involved in one stage or another of the wild animal business
know very little about animals. So I concentrate on keeping in
touch with everybody important in the business, because while
they may know nothing about animals, they do know something
about people. And despite the cliché "familiarity breeds contempt,"

it is important in the wild animal business to know and to have confidence in the people involved: Having confidence in another person is more than half the battle in any business. I assure people who know nothing about animals, "Don't worry. Zeehandelaar will take care of you. No Wall Street mongers are in on this." They invariably seem to like this approach—and have had little cause to regret their trust in my know-how. Everybody in the wild animal business knows me. And not all the people in the animal business like me—some even hate me. But that's all right, just as long as they talk about me I am going to get action.

Naturally I do a bit of speaking to people involved in the exhibit end of the wild animal business. In the past ten years I have delivered speeches at banquets and conventions of organized zoo people all over the world. It has become almost habitual at these conventions to have several staple attractions. The first is a trading session, at which each zoo describes the excess animals it has for sale, or airs its needs; and the second is my speech. And while freely admitting I need the services of a book-writer to present my story, I, like the late Chauncey Depew, need no such thing when it comes to my speeches. Here my listeners are subjected to unadulterated Zeehandelaarisms.

Instead of offering choice excerpts from my past speeches, it might be more fun to discuss some of the people compelled to listen to them. Invariably many of these zoo people know very little about animals.

8.
The Zoo People

A zoo, of course, is a hierarchy; and it didn't take too long for a certain professor to determine the reason things almost always go wrong with any hierarchy: Employees tend to rise to their highest level of incompetence. By enlarging on this basic principle, the professor, Lawrence J. Peter, (aided by coauthor Raymond Hull), produced a best-seller. Although there is no specific mention of zoo operations in this avidly read book (*The Peter Principle*), its quips and corollaries are as appropriate for zoos as they are for other forms of hierarchy. In fact from what I have observed and experienced in dealing with zoo people it is apparently true that most of the effective work is performed by people on the lower rungs of the ladder, who have not yet been elevated to their proper level of incompetence.

Normally there are about nineteen categories of people involved in the line and staff organization of a large zoo, and these are:

1. PRESIDENT, ZOOLOGICAL SOCIETY
2. VICE-PRESIDENT, ZOOLOGICAL SOCIETY
3. EXECUTIVE DIRECTOR, ZOOLOGICAL SOCIETY
4. PARKS COMMISSIONER

5. DIRECTOR OF PARKS
6. SUPERINTENDENT OF PARKS
7. ZOO DIRECTOR
8. ASSISTANT ZOO DIRECTOR
9. ASSOCIATE ASSISTANT ZOO DIRECTOR
10. GENERAL CURATOR
11. DEPARTMENT CURATORS
12. ASSISTANT CURATORS
13. ZOO VETERINARIAN
14. ZOOLOGIST
15. ZOO DIETICIAN
16. PUBLICITY DIRECTOR
17. HEAD KEEPER
18. ASSISTANT HEAD KEEPER
19. ZOO KEEPERS

Prof. Dr. Heinz-Georg Klös (first row standing, left) West Berlin Zoo Director, hosts American Zoo professionals.

Because all these titles involve duties with various levels of responsibility in the care and protection of wild animals in captivity, it might be fun to compare the people themselves with their allegorical counterparts in the wild animal kingdom, as follows:

PRESIDENT OF THE ZOOLOGICAL SOCIETY
> He can be compared to the king of all the beasts. At least in his opinion he thinks so. Therefore, he could be classed as a *Lion*.

VICE-PRESIDENT OF THE ZOOLOGICAL SOCIETY
> He can be regarded as the substitute king of all the beasts. Occasionally he believes himself to actually be the king. He behaves like a lion and tries to look like one, but he must be classed as a *Mountain Lion*.

EXECUTIVE DIRECTOR OF THE ZOOLOGICAL SOCIETY
> A most domineering—and dominating—person. Like the executive officer on a battleship entering the U-boat area, he growls and scowls. He may be likened to a *Grizzly Bear*.

PARKS COMMISSIONER
> He is a man who visits the zoo as often as once a year—and makes that visit with record speed. In fact, many observers believe him to be the fastest official in the field since he has such a vast territory to worry about. For his speed he can be likened to a *Cheetah*.

DIRECTOR OF PARKS
> He is always worried about such insensitive things as litter, refuse, maintenance, cleaning, etc. Over the

years he has become known as the man who wants
everybody to "keep their stuff in a sack, or bag."
For our purposes he can be relegated to the marsupials
and called a *Kangaroo.*

SUPERINTENDENT OF PARKS

Similar to the director of parks but in a minor manner;
and so he can be classified as a *Wallaroo.*

ZOO DIRECTOR

By all means he is the wisest person in the zoo. He is
the know-it-all with unusual activity during the night
hours, while occasionally shouting in the daytime.
It would be proper to categorize him as a *Great
Horned Owl.*

ASSISTANT ZOO DIRECTOR

Basically he reflects the same attributes as the zoo
director but is more vulnerable because he may be used
as both the object of a buck-pass and as the person to
blame when trouble comes. Slightly more active and
slightly more human than his superior, the assistant
Z.D. has to have equal energy both night and day, so
he can be called an *Owl Monkey.*

ASSOCIATE ASSISTANT ZOO DIRECTOR

This man is usually angry at his title because he
believes he is more zoo director than assistant zoo
director. And because he does a lot of shouting at
all times, he can be labeled a *Screech Owl.*

GENERAL CURATOR

He is an extremely difficult person to classify.
Since he is an in-between kind of creature he might be
put into the egg-laying mammal group and called a
Platypus.

DEPARTMENT CURATORS

Here are the curators of mammals, birds, reptiles, fish and whatnot—all fighting for a lion's share of the zoo's acquisition budget so that their continued employ can be warranted. Since these people are real fighters, it is fitting to class them as *Hyenas.*

ASSISTANT CURATORS

They have the same qualifications and aims as the curators, but their purpose is two-sided: (1) to make a lot of fuss about nothing so zoo people know they exist, and (2) to take the blame for trouble arising from wrong decisions by the curators. So assistant curators can be called *Prairie Dogs.*

ZOO VETERINARIAN

This professional is an emphatic person who looks at animals as if they were humans and he were a physician. He also acts as a Homo sapiens when dealing with distressed keepers. Since he is very human and full of tricks, he can best be called a *Chimpanzee.*

ZOOLOGIST

This studious product of academe is a man of books. His nose is often damaged by being buried in learned papers, magazines, and books. Invariably his proboscis is pressed against the panes of indoor exhibits when it is not buried in reading matter. Since his nose seems to be his leading attribute, it is fitting to class this gentleman as a *Nose Monkey.*

ZOO DIETICIAN

This scientist knows all about food and drink. He wines and dines the animal kingdom under his responsibility whether they want the food or not. What the animals refuse to eat or drink this researcher will have to sample himself. He should have a very strong stomach with the capacity to readily accept leftovers. Therefore, it is proper to classify him a *Wolverine*.

PUBLICITY DIRECTOR

This aggressive person is an indefatigable drum-beater who has to be heard loud and clear—especially by the press. Generally it doesn't matter much to him whether he is right or wrong, whether what he is communicating to the papers is true or false. The important thing is that he is heard—and makes everyone who hears him remember that his zoo is still there and hasn't been condemned by the city for urban housing developments. Properly so, he can be dubbed a *Siamang*.

HEAD KEEPER

One of the important items in the backbone of any zoo, this valuable man oversees the entire daily routine of the keepers. Burdened by blame from his superiors and harassed by complaints from his subordinates he must have a broad back and a long neck. It is most appropriate to classify him, therefore, a *Giraffe*.

ASSISTANT HEAD KEEPER

Obviously this man has to have a double disposition. He must be as qualified as the head keeper so he can assume command in the head keeper's absence. And he must take the blame from the head keeper when the head keeper gets blamed. Since he, too, must have a broad back and a long neck—but on a lesser scale— it is proper to call him a giraffe gazelle, or *Gerenuk*.

ZOO KEEPERS

Since these people render daily care to the zoo's animals it is understandable that they can be called busy *Beavers*.

Obviously—with at least nineteen varieties of Homo sapiens looking after hundreds of different species of mammals, reptiles, and birds—there are bound to be flaws and friction. But to further project our animal allegory, it is interesting to visualize a combination of the chimpanzee (the veterinarian), the giraffe (the head keeper), and the great horned owl (the zoo director) moving in unison.

The chimpanzee rides on the back of the giraffe and the great horned owl perches atop the giraffe's head. In this manner the trio moves around the zoo—with dignity, superiority, power, and authority. But if the head keeper (giraffe) makes one false step, or stumbles while striking an obstacle, he may very well fall, taking the zoo director and the veterinarian with him whether they like it or not.

In retrospect, the zoo keepers (busy beavers) are among the most dedicated—and busiest—people in any zoo. Assuredly they do not follow their selfless careers for money, because zoo keepers can hardly consider themselves rich on their salaries. Yet these quiet workers, who are rarely appreciated by the public, seem to find fulfillment in working with animals.

On an August morning before exhibit hours I happened to enter a city zoo to visit the director. As I walked past the lion house the big cats were stretched out seemingly lifeless in the muggy morning heat. One Siberian tiger drew my attention because he looked just like a hunter's trophy spread on the floor of a rich man's hunting lodge.

Suddenly the cat came to life. It actually reared up on its hind legs and went into a sort of dance, while mewing like a kitten. Out of the corner of my eye I spied a khaki-clad keeper, dragging a water hose, approaching the tiger's cage. In no time at all the keeper was dousing the big cat from head to foot with a powerful stream of water—and the cat danced as if delirious with joy while he was thoroughly drenched. It was easy to tell this keeper had great empathy for his charge. Indeed, there was a bond between beast and keeper bordering upon love.

On another day I watched a keeper feeding cicadas to a diversified group of amphibians housed in a large exhibit. How expertly he spread the insects to all points of the cage so that each amphibian could trap its prey in a natural way!

From years of personal observation I have found that the keepers are the "muscles" in any zoo. These are the people who always try to make their animals comfortable—to make the beasts happy if you will—and to see that they receive food properly and are in good health. In certain cases the keepers' jobs are quite dangerous: On occasion they can lose an arm, a leg, or even their lives in doing their job—if they forget to take proper precautions.

If the keepers are the muscles of the zoo, who is the backbone?

I feel it is a trio: (1) the veterinarian, (2) the head keeper, and (3) the zoo director. Since veterinarians deserve a book about themselves, and since head keepers are generally zoo keepers who are in that exalted position because of seniority, I intend to comment at length only about zoo directors.

One of the most famous zoo directors in all history was the late John Tee-Van of the Bronx Zoo. He worked in his teens as an artist for the zoo and remained to direct it years later. He literally grew up in the zoo and was eventually familiar with everything and everyone connected with the zoo, including its animal inhabitants.

Most modern zoo directors are not of the breed of Mr. Tee-Van. Many of them are zoologists who have made a career in administering a big business. (Today any city-owned zoo or zoo operated by a zoological association has indeed become a big business.) The zoo director is beset with personnel problems, with budgetary problems, with political problems, and with the human problem of trying to keep his job. Frankly the zoo director today is so busy he hardly ever gets a chance to enjoy, or see, the animals whose well-being he is charged with.

The zoo director is rarely subjected to personal danger, although I still remember the case of a very young zoo director who was overcome by vertigo while in the reptile house and collapsed against a pane of glass that fronted a display of an African bushmaster. The glass shattered and the director's hand fell into the display area near the venomous snake. In a wink the snake struck. Regrettably, the zoo director died in short order.

Although few zoo directors purposely endanger themselves—or even accidentally run the risk of being injured—there are cases where the actions of such supposedly intelligent administrators have endangered the lives and the well-being of their animal charges.

Several years ago a zoo director ordered an especially wild kind of zebra. This remarkably skittish and sensitive animal required special handling after arrival at the zoo. I wrote to the director in this regard, and told him that when the zebra arrived it would be accustomed to being confined in a crate for months. Therefore, he should not release the animal into an outdoor enclosure upon arrival at the zoo. Instead I suggested the crate be placed in a darkened, small room and the zebra released into this room. "After a few days," I wrote, "take the zebra and lead him into a larger, brighter room so he can become gradually accustomed to freedom." If the beast were docile after a few days in the large room it could safely be released into an outdoor corral. Maybe the zoo director was piqued at my written lecture about how to handle a wild zebra. But the facts are that no sooner did the truck bearing the zebra to this zoo arrive than the director had the crate placed in the center of a large field enclosed by a wire fence—and he ordered the zebra released!

Immediately the crazed beast hurled itself against the wire fence and killed itself. Regrettably my insurance on the animal had ended the moment the animal was dropped at the zoo. Why the director didn't follow my instructions will never be known, but what is known is that he lost a bundle of the zoo's budget by disregarding my suggestions. Yes. The zoo director is indeed like the great horned owl, but on occasion doesn't display this species' wisdom.

One last species must be considered in any animal allegory related to zoo operations. Although this "animal" is not part of the zoo's management or labor force, his activities necessarily influence—and perhaps at times interfere with—zoo operations. And this person, the wild animal dealer, can be classified as a *Chameleon.*

The animal dealer must be able to laugh or cry, rest or jump, give or take. He must be nimble enough to adjust himself lightning-like to any emergency and protect himself with camouflage from attack on all sides. Undoubtedly the animal dealer is the most controversial figure in the zoo-world; but he is also the man most easily spared. At times he is tolerated; at other times, praised; or despised by the very same client. The animal dealer changes with the zoo's political weather—and assumes any color necessary to please his client and protect himself at the same time. Indeed, the animal dealer in many ways often emulates the chameleon.

No giraffe—with or without the assistance of the great horned owl and/or chimpanzee—can ever catch the chameleon. Therefore this species will survive regardless whether he is liked or disliked by zoo officials—and will turn up when needed. More than one hundred years ago the famous French author Jules Verne predicted man would travel to the moon. Three American space pioneers fulfilled this vision. George Orwell, in his famous book *Animal Farm,* described the behavior of animals in a world taken over by the animals. Chameleon Zeehandelaar, in this book, theorizes on what would happen if all the people running a specific zoo were to die on the same day, leaving the animals in charge. How would they make out?

In the meantime, while men are still in charge, zoo directors are constantly faced with the problem of maintaining their exhibits, replenishing the existing supply of animal inventory within their domains, and acquiring rare animals to attract attention and public interest. In olden times, zoos were accustomed to finance expeditions into safari country to bring back specimens for exhibit. But when modern zoos require rare specimens— especially birds and animals behind the Iron and the Bamboo curtains—they generally use the services of a wild animal dealer.

9.
Behind the Curtains

Many years ago one of my clients wanted to buy some Soviet animals. Since this was my first experience with the people behind the Iron Curtain I foolishly decided to make my request in their mother tongue. So I looked up a Russian translator living in Manhattan who possessed one of the five typewriters—in all of New York City—with Russian type.

At no great expense, but with genuine anxiety, I finally managed to mail a three-page letter—typed in Russian—which presumably reflected my desires, and which I signed with trepidation; because I could neither read nor understand what I was signing.

About a month later I received a reply from Mr. Big at the Moscow Zoo-Centre informing me my letter was not clear, and would I please restate my wishes in English so that they could understand them. From that time on, I have done a brisk business behind the Iron Curtain by using only English.

The first thing I found out about doing business with the Russians is they are not interested in American cash. All the animal deals we have had involved swapping specimens. A typical deal of this type occurred some years back in connection with the importation

of a pair of very rare—and very gentle—freshwater seals from
Siberia for the New York Aquarium. Because these seals come
from Lake Baikal they are aptly called Baikal seals. This is the
only species of fresh-water seal anywhere in the world, and upon
arrival in New York City they were the only seals of this species
exhibited in North America.

But before the Soviets shipped these seals to America I had
to send them two sea lions, one ostrich, and ten toucans. After
my animals arrived safely in Moscow, the Soviets shipped their
seals to me. Comfortingly, in the deals we have done during the
past decade or more, there have been no reneges on the part of
the Soviet suppliers.

In October 1962 I decided to make a business visit to the Soviet
Union. Contrary to popular belief, doing business with the USSR
is perfectly legal, and encouraged by our Government. It is also
permissible for Americans to visit the Soviet Union without any
special permit. All that is necessary is a passport, and, of course,
the permission of the USSR in the form of visa.

Visitor's visas are issued by Intourist, the Soviet tourist
organization in New York City, while business visas are issued
only by the Soviet Embassy in Washington. It takes from three to
four weeks for a visitor's visa to be processed; and the time it
takes for a business visa to be cleared is altogether indefinite and
unpredictable. Knowing this it didn't make sense to go through
the ordinary red-tape channels of obtaining a visa. Besides, my
sudden urge to visit the Soviet Union occurred during a visit to
the Netherlands.

From Amsterdam I cabled the Moscow director of the Soviet
Zoo-Centre to ask if he would be willing to see me. One hour
after my cable went off I received a long-distance call from
Moscow instructing me (in a most friendly fashion) precisely how
to proceed.

Feeling a bit like the hero in *Thunderball,* I followed these
instructions. The following day I rushed off to the Soviet Trade
Delegation in Amsterdam. But not a single soul at this delegation

knew anything at all about the purpose of my visit, and I was speedily shown the door. Upon returning to my hotel, my Dutch temper was simmering. But no sooner had I entered my room than the phone rang. It was the Soviet trade delegate to the Netherlands, himself. After some soothing apologies on his part, I was back at the mansion again. Twenty minutes after my second appearance at this stately mansion in the heart of the city, I was once more on the way back to my hotel. But this time I had a visa—with instructions to enter the USSR within three days and to depart within a week from my arrival.

I left Amsterdam the next morning via KLM for Moscow. My arrival at the Moscow airport seemed a portent of things to come: miserable rain-and-fog weather, and unusual cold. Somehow, as the plane rolled to a dead stop, I felt an end to all enjoyment. And when two mysterious immigration officers planted themselves at the plane door, immediately confiscated my passport, and stared at me as if I were a man from Mars, I actually felt half-dead.

Suddenly they said, "Welcome to Moscow." And I almost answered, "Who you kidding." But prudently I remained silent. With that they arranged themselves on either side of me and politely escorted me toward the government inspection facility. At that checkpoint no less than six men approached me. In unison, two of my interrogators asked: "Are you a tourist?" Since I was not wearing a camera the answer should have been obvious, but I managed to squeak out a "No." Another pair asked what kind of firearms I carried. A bit more warmly I answered, "None." The last pair turned out to be the Assistant Director of the Moscow Zoo-Centre and his assistant, whose title I then did not understand and still don't.

Magically, from the moment I was turned over to these engaging individuals, everything changed for the better. The clouds vanished and the sun came out. Almost immediately my passport was returned. My single suitcase (I always travel light) was not opened for inspection. And I found myself ensconced comfortably in a huge black limousine heading for a hotel.

The Leningradskaya turned out to be an excellent—and new—hotel with luxurious accommodations. The Assistant Director, my host, spoke German fluently—and seemed to fall all over himself with gratitude for my visit. He earnestly wanted to learn all he could about Western zoos, because, like 99 percent of the Soviet citizenry, he was prohibited from visiting any Western countries. Although my host was a Communist party member, his status as a government official in the hierarchial ladder evidently was not high enough to permit such special privileges as touring foreign zoos at Soviet expense.

Meanwhile, I inadvertently managed to meet the Soviet people face-to-face.

My hotel was newly furnished and quite comfortable, but the only major deficiency was its elevators. Narrow, hot, and strange-smelling, the cabs of these inadequate lifts crawled skyward at a speed 1/25 that of an adult tortoise. One day, when the elevator I was in suddenly got stuck between floors for nineteen minutes, I managed to get real close to the Soviet people. Looking back, I must have lost nineteen pounds right then and there.

A more pleasant experience was the welcome dinner in my honor provided by the Zoo-Centre Assistant Director.

At this unforgettable affair, the varied courses, the many liquors, and the unimaginably slow service combined to consume all of three hours. Imagine. There I was, Zeehandelaar, the zoo-handler, who *never* takes more than ten minutes to eat any meal, stuck at a dining table for *three whole hours*. Believe me, the change was welcome; and the vodka (most powerful I have ever downed) worked wonders.

Who can blame me for feeling that this sumptuous spread would be the last culinary treat the Soviets had in store for me during my visit? But to my complete surprise I was treated to the very same kind of three-hour dinner each and every evening during my Moscow visit.

With adequate coaching from my ever-attentive host, I became quite expert in recognizing the different kinds of vodka served at the dinners; and memorized the various entrees and desserts as well. In retrospect I don't know whether to attribute this to my penchant for memorizing trivia, or to the frenetic efforts of my host, who took great pains as we swallowed glass after glass of the powerful stuff to point out the remarkable attributes of the liquor that made tomato juice an international best-seller.

At October's end Moscow resembles any major Western city. Crowds jam the streets. Despite the occasionally unfamiliar clothes, the people look just like October noon-time crowds on Fifth Avenue. But the animated bustle of Christmas shoppers is absent. Also absent in Moscow are the exciting store windows lining both sides of Fifth Avenue.

But if the Moscow surface is not as engaging or as enjoyable as Fifth Avenue in the fall, there is no comparison between Moscow life below the street and life in the New York subway.

The Moscow subway defies description; I don't mind admitting it was one of the most amazing things I have ever seen. The subway consists of a sequence of stations—all lined with solid marble. Each station is a unique museum—with paintings, sculpture, tapestry, murals, etc. My host seemed immeasurably pleased when I purposely left the train at every station and marveled at both architecture and art. I stared for perhaps fifteen minutes at the art in each station, but I wish time would have permitted me a day in each place.

As for the trains—in contrast to the New York City subway— the Moscow cars are spotless, fast, on time, and announce arrival at each station. The passengers are generally silent: 99 percent read books.

Above ground, the streets are often as wide as turnpikes. Fifty percent of the vehicles seem to be taxis, and most of the other vehicles (cars and trucks) seem to be in the service of the Soviet Government. Slicing through the moving mass of vehicles are streetcars and trolley buses. And sprinkled heavily along the right of way, an army of female street cleaners wield witch-like brooms. Here and there moving hulks of motorized equipment, manned by female drivers, repair the street surfaces.

Since my visit took place several weeks before the celebration of the November Revolution, giant-sized pictures of Soviet heroes and officials hung from the buildings, overshadowing almost everything else. The buildings seemed wrapped in enormous red banners and flags. It seemed rather strange to me that people would permit themselves to be so inundated with such a systemized approach to a celebration. In a way, the force of successful political activism exuded everywhere. It was a relief for me, who scrupulously avoids politics in any shape or form, to quit Red Square and return to zoo business.

All animal export, import, exchange, or trade inside the USSR is handled exclusively by the Moscow Zoo-Centre. Moreover, all catching, propagating, and operation of all game reserves are handled and supervised by that efficient agency. No wild animal in captivity can move from one point to another inside the Soviet Union unless its movements have been arranged for by the Zoo-Centre. And, of course, no animal can be shipped out of the Soviet Union without permission of this authority. Oddly enough, in connection with the capture of wild animals, the Zoo-Centre is *not* the ultimate authority. If I need a markhor, which to satisfy my contract must be caught in Siberia, the Zoo-Centre would need the permission of a local Siberian game warden before confirming the order to me. But it is readily understandable that in a country where local agencies must unquestioningly cooperate with national ones, the Zoo-Centre wields a unique amount of authority and influence.

Dr. Shilaev, Director at that time, is an elderly man who speaks and writes only in Russian. But this aged gentleman happens to have a female secretary—by no means bad-looking and certainly of breeding age—who, like a pet cheetah, appeared from nowhere precisely when needed; and regrettably disappeared into nowhere much too quickly. This apparently indispensable specimen of Soviet femininity spoke English fluently: She naturally acted as my interpreter during talks with the Zoo-Centre's personnel.

I possess a vast collection of books about wild animals in my New Rochelle office. Many of these references are long since out of print, but by religiously reading these books I have trained myself to be a walking encyclopedia of wild animal names, facts, and feats. I frankly confess that if I were blessed with such a secretary I would not need to own a single reference work for my business. I am convinced that that lovely lady could describe every animal in every genus—with the Latin nomenclature—and furnish facts and figures going back 500 years!

To make her mental achievements even more astonishing, she can present this mass of information retrieval in at least six languages. In short this talented secretary could be a priceless possession for any American zoo, or for the office of the AAZPA too. Candidly, I now confess I wanted to urge her to defect. But since I am not equipped with the physical attributes of the leader of TV's *Mission: Impossible,* I failed to summon up the courage to make such a proposal. Yet ever since fate made me meet her, I have hoped by some miracle she will someday show up in New Rochelle and announce that she is ready to be my new secretary. Meanwhile, rest assured that if anyone—including yours truly—receives communications from the Soviet Union about wild animals, the messages are probably prepared by this gifted lady.

After several conferences with people at the Zoo-Centre I reluctantly left this lady's presence to visit the Moscow Zoo.

Guided by the Assistant Director of the Moscow Zoo-Centre, I found that the zoo itself is divided into two equal areas by a very busy thoroughfare. Having paid admission to one area, the visitor is handed an admission pass to the other area. But one has to be brave, to say the least; because abandoning one area to visit the other is quite dangerous, due to the traffic.

Naturally I was quite interested in all the animals on exhibit, and the manner in which they were displayed. The giant panda drew me like a magnet. To my horror I found that rare beast in a very old feline building, in an ancient cage with thick iron bars, sandwiched between a spotted hyena on its left and a Florida bobcat on its right. Evidently the position of honor in the zoo reflects political significance, because the most prominent display was a litter of *Tigris styani* (Southern Chinese tigers), which at that time were the only specimens on exhibit outside of China. A truly magnificent animal—somewhere in size between the Bengal and the Siberian tiger—the Southern Chinese tiger boasts a remarkably reddish-brown coat, not too well striped. At the time of my visit, the litter, consisting of two males and one female, was four months old and had been separated from its mother. The Moscow Zoo also displayed an unbelievably large pair of Manchurian tiger (*Tigris amurensis*), the male of which must have weighed at least 800 pounds.

I noticed as I walked past the exhibits that some Soviet children were feeding two very large walruses. Each child proffered a single fish and the walruses gently grabbed the fish with obvious relish. I asked my guide why the zoo didn't feed their walruses the same kind of diet that this species enjoys in captivity in St. Louis. And my host, confessing ignorance, asked, "What kind of diet is that?" And I answered, "Clams smothered in whipped cream."

Without batting an eyelash he explained that in Moscow clams are rather difficult to find, whipped cream is far too capitalistic, and communist walruses are accustomed to more spartan treatment than American walruses. Moreover, he continued, walruses would hardly encounter whipped cream in their natural habitat.

The most impressive birds in the Moscow Zoo are the Manchurian cranes. These rare birds are virtually impossible to import into America. When I expressed my amazement at the sight of these rare specimens, my guide casually asked, "Why are you so amazed? After all, these are nothing but common Manchurian cranes." If I had false teeth, I would either have dropped them or swallowed them after this remark.

The zoo itself is very old. As a matter of courtesy it suffices to say that the Moscow Zoo cannot compare favorably in plant and layout with most American zoos. It resembles an old zoo in Western Europe: old buildings, old enclosures, and a mixed-up mish-mash of animals crowded together like a free-for-all. Some Siberian hoofstock climb on huge rocks found throughout the zoo; and in those cases visitors using field glasses see the exhibits more effectively than they could with the naked eye.

All hoofstock originating from any point in the Soviet Union must be quarantined for thirty days at a station near the Moscow airport. This adds a month from the time the animal is caught and collected until it leaves the USSR. To understand the time-lags in importing Soviet animals, consider the case of an ibex.

If I order an ibex from Siberia, it must be shipped to Moscow via the Trans-Siberian Railroad. This trip takes from ten to fourteen days after my order has been approved by the Zoo-Centre. Upon arrival in Moscow, my ibex is quarantined for thirty days. Because of American quarantine requirements, the animal must then be shipped to Hamburg for a sixty-day quarantine. And when the ibex finally arrives in America, it, of course, must be quarantined at Clifton, New Jersey.

Meanwhile, Zeehandelaar dollars have been tied up in animals previously shipped to the Soviets in exchange for the ibex. And it will take me almost six months from the time the ibex is approved for shipment in order to recoup.

A trauma of this sort occurred in 1962 when I shipped a load of sea lions and other American animals to the Moscow Zoo-Centre. The sea lions were caught off the California coast just in time to make a flight arranged by Air Express International. The animals were flown over the Pole to Copenhagen and through the Iron Curtain to the Soviet capital. Only after their arrival did Moscow authorize the largest shipment of saiga antelopes (*Saiga tartarica*) ever exported to this country.

Then after the quarantine in Moscow, the quarantine in Hamburg, and the quarantine in Clifton these magnificent specimens were shipped to all corners of our country by my firm. One male and four females were delivered to the National

Zoological Park in Washington; one male and two females went to the Toledo Zoo, and the same assortment of antelopes went to the zoo in San Francisco. Two females were shipped to Dallas to be mates for a male already at this Texas zoo, and a female joined the pair already in residence at the Philadelphia Zoo. A pair was also shipped to the San Diego Zoo, but tragedy struck and one animal died soon after arrival.

Obviously the American zoos ordered these Soviet creatures in order to attempt to breed them successfully here in the United States. While the saiga is one of the most common antelopes in its wild state in the USSR (more than 3,000,000 reportedly roam the tundra), it is rare and delicate in captivity in the Western world. The longevity record is seven years in an American zoo.

In any event, the animals that come from behind the Iron Curtain are nearly always desirable and practically impossible to obtain. We as Americans should feel almost lucky to get these animals whenever we can.

An exception to this statement was made about three years ago. At that time I cabled an inquiry to Moscow about the price of twenty-four Brent geese (twelve males and twelve females). I did not place any order, but merely asked for a quotation and the terms of the customary swap agreement. To my surprise, I received no reply. Whether or not the efficient female in the Zoo-Centre office had been replaced by a less efficient person I, of course, could not know, but having received no reply to my cable I naturally assumed the Soviets lacked interest in such a deal—and promptly forgot the entire matter.

Several months later—and precisely on the very day Aeroflot was scheduled to arrive at Kennedy to inaugurate Moscow-to-New York flights—I received a cable from Moscow informing me that the twenty-four geese I had "ordered" would arrive the following day, on the second Aeroflot flight.

What was I to do?

I had given the Soviets no order. I did not have customers ready to receive these geese, despite the fact that these birds were very desirable. Moreover, I did not know what the Soviets wanted for their birds—which animals I would be obligated to deliver if I accepted the geese. But believe me, in this instance financial considerations were secondary. Little did the Soviets realize that due to Department of Agriculture regulations no Russian geese could be landed in America without a permit. And if Aeroflot would have come down at Kennedy with a cargo of geese, and without such a permit, agents of the USDA would have quarantined the plane, its passengers, and crew as soon as the ship had rolled to a stop.

While inwardly convulsed at the complications which would have resulted, I could hardly help thinking, "what if the birds had been on the first Aeroflot flight and the USDA had impounded the dignitaries aboard of both nations?" To avert the possibility of a nasty international incident I immediately cabled back to Moscow telling them I had never ordered any geese, but had only asked for a quotation. I also acidly pointed out they had better cancel the impending shipment, or else. I immediately phoned our concerned agencies about the possible arrival of illicit geese; and disavowed having anything to do with the birds if they landed in error at Kennedy. Luckily for all concerned, the Soviets apparently canceled the shipment—because the birds never arrived.

Although I have cable contact behind the Iron Curtain, and have, on occasion visited the Soviet Union, I cannot honestly claim the same kind of contacts behind the Bamboo Curtain.

Until the end of 1969 trading with the Communist Chinese (except for small amounts of money) had been taboo for decades. And ironically the world's most sought-after wild animal specimen, the giant panda, originates within the confines of the Bamboo Curtain. Although I was the only person in the United States with a valid license to import a giant panda (worth about $50,000 delivered here), the rules have recently been changed by the Administration relaxing restrictions on Chinese wild animal imports which are not for resale. But despite relaxation of regulations, aside from the London Zoo's acquisition of Chi-Chi, no zoo or wild animal dealer has been successful in obtaining a specimen for exhibit purposes. I am trying to contact someone behind the Bamboo Curtain who can facilitate such a deal, but so far have come up with nothing but promises. I am willing to pay cash, to swap animals, or do whatever the Chinese might desire— within reason—to effect the importation of such a sorely needed acquisition for our American zoory.

If the Communist Chinese someday consent to sell a giant panda to an American zoo through my ministrations, the problem of mutual trust will probably arise. Would I first ship them animals in hopes of collecting the panda later, as I customarily do with Soviet deals? I have had experience with the Russians, and they have never defaulted. Since I have had no experience in business dealing with the Communist Chinese it would seem prudent to have their animal placed in escrow first at a neutral country's zoo before I sent my swap animals in. At this writing, the entire project is in its imaginative stages. Normally I cross bridges only when I come to them; but in this case, like Bernard Baruch, I like to lay down some pontoons first. Which is precisely what I am doing now. Whether or not I will be successful in someday importing a giant panda from behind the Bamboo Curtain still remains to be seen, but the challenge lives with me everyday.

10.
The Pet Fanciers

Some Americans are so fascinated with representatives of the wild animal kingdom that they have surrounded themselves with unusual pets and game preserves. Such people can be labeled "private animal fanciers."

Someday psychologists or psychiatrists may undertake in-depth studies of what makes affluent Americans want to raise lion cubs as pets, or for that matter cheetahs and chimpanzees. What motivates millionaires in America to transplant a representative of the African veldt or the Australian outback to areas of the land of the free and the taxed? Because most of my time in the wild animal business has been devoted to self-education in understanding the motives of the various kinds of people in the business, I have hardly had time to critically examine or even reflect on the reasons that motivate pet fanciers to act the way they do. I sincerely hope some psychologist or psychiatrist who reads this book will proceed with some serious work in this direction.

Meanwhile, it is fitting to provide some groundwork in animal behavior before examining the bizarre people who keep wild animals as pets.

Frankly there is no such miracle as a tame wild animal. Tame actually defines a relationship between a wild animal and a human being. If the animal does not harm the human it is considered "tame." The popular definition of a tame animal is a wild animal which will not attack or injure human beings. But there is never any certainty in labeling any wild animal "tame," because it may or may not live up to this definition. For example a cheetah that is the pet of an Oriental potentate may be quite tame with her master, but quite vicious with anybody else. I have seen an allegedly tame cheetah left with a local veterinarian while her master went off on holiday. Upon the master's return several weeks later, the cheetah seemed to have completely forgotten him; because when her master approached, the cat leaped on him and clawed him terribly. And so I reiterate, a wild animal is always a wild animal. It can never be considered completely tame and must always be handled with care. However, because of their intelligence, wild animals can be *trained.*

In this regard the animals are trained to perform certain tricks or acts. They have been motivated by various drives such as hunger and fear in order to be molded into pliable, and obedient subjects for their trainers. But again, even a trained animal cannot be expected to perform properly with anyone other than the person who actually trained it. Books are filled with stories of circus animals that went bersek, or suddenly attacked their trainers, or went after certain individuals for whom they had acquired a hate. The facts and the stories support my theory that a wild animal is that way forever—whether tame or trained.

The facts also indicate that wild animals (like people) sometimes "go off their rocker" by being subjected to captivity. I clearly recall the case of a wealthy fancier who went off to Africa on safari. For some silly reason, best known to him, this wealthy dilettante of wildlife returned to America cuddling a lion cub, which he thought he could rear into Simba, *a la* Tarzan. Little larger than a kitten when captured, the cub eagerly lapped up bottled milk from his master's hand, and actually slept in his master's stateroom on the return voyage to the States. But by the time the ship eased into its berth in New York City, something seemed drastically wrong with the cub. Its master managed, surreptitiously to slip the cub into a suite at the Pierre Hotel, but no sooner did it land upon the carpet than the lion cub began to walk backwards. It refused to move forward or to the side—only backwards. And no amount of coaxing could change the cub's direction. Alarmed, the lion's master phoned me in New Rochelle and explained his pet's strange behavior. He sounded so desperate I invited him to bring the cub to New Rochelle to be examined by my veterinarian.

The very same evening my lion-loving friend arrived, cuddling his cub. He eyed the cat with all the concern of a banker whose teen-age son suddenly turns up with a far-away look in his eye, wearing bell-bottoms. My veterinarian who has years of experience with both big and little cats, examined the lion cub thoroughly, but couldn't come up with any explanation for the beast's insistence on walking backwards. Since the cub seemed in otherwise good health I suggested to the animal fancier that he go along with this aberration. But I assured him if this unique habit became annoying, I could find a zoo which would welcome a backwards-walking lion. He reacted to my advice as if I had

F.J. Zeehandelaar and son David with Lion Cub that traveled only in reverse. (*Macy Westchester Newspapers*)

suggested he turn Little Eva over to Simon Legree, and returned to New York in a huff. But to his dismay he ran into further trouble.

As he entered the Pierre lobby—with the cub's head protruding from his cashmere coat—the pet fancier was stopped by the hotel security, who gently told him that the Pierre rented accommodations only for humans, but had no facilities for baby lions.

Regrettably I never learned what happened to the wrong-way walking cub, because a neurotic elephant soon occupied my attention.

A Pennsylvania pet fancier, who was not turned on enough by raising Black Angus beef, decided a baby elephant would be nice to have on the farm. He ordered a baby Indian elephant that was less than four feet high at the shoulder when the ship bearing it to this country docked at Charleston, South Carolina. By chance I met the ship and watched the elephant unloaded, led docilely to a truck, and installed for the long ride to Pennsylvania. What happened psychologically to this poor elephant during the ride will never be known. But no sooner had the beast been unloaded at my customer's farm than it began walking around in a circle. No matter what its keeper (an American farmhand, understandably a poor substitute for an Indian mahout) did, the elephant insisted on walking round and around. Shortly after its arrival, the elephant quickened its pace. A few days later it began to run round and around, faster and faster in a tight circle—and suddenly dropped dead. The autopsy indicated heart failure. What made this animal suddenly go crazy has never been determined.

Even though my name, telephone number, and address are not in the Manhattan *Yellow Pages* I am still annoyed almost every working day by the American public. Almost daily I receive calls from bird fanciers who want one parrot, or one Australian cockatoo, or a mynah bird, or a toucan. Sometimes I get a call for a python that some ambitious young lady desires to train as a dancing partner. Or children call to ask me if I will buy turtles and frogs. By now it should be clearly understood that Zeehandelaar is not a retailer, but rather a wholesaler who mainly supplies zoos which cannot supply themselves.

I do, however, supply the wants of private people who order animals in more than retail quantities. Such exceptions include the American millionaires who maintain game preserves on the vast lands they own.

The earliest American known to have maintained his own preserve stocked with foreign game was the late John Murray Forbes, father of William Hathaway Forbes, first president of what is now AT&T. In the nineteenth century Forbes stocked his island off Wood's Hole, Massachusetts, with wild boar, European stags and does, and English pheasant and grouse. In a wonderfully methodical way he attempted to duplicate Robin Hood's forest. He even transplanted beech trees and English evergreens in order to create a natural environment for the game he imported. His purpose, I suppose, was to present a suitably stocked preserve for the hunting pleasures of family and friends visiting his feudal island.

In certain parts of the Southwest, where the climate is similar to the African veldt, great game preserves have been established with the primary purpose of providing natural homes for varieties of African, Australian, and Asian animals. The preserve owner feels he will provide a natural haven for the rapidly dwindling population of world wildlife. He believes—and rightly so—that if he is successful in propagating the stock that roams about the preserve in a natural fashion, he is helping to conserve and add to the ecological balance of the whole world.

In August 1968 I decided to journey down to San Antonio, Texas, to attend a Pan-American animal health meeting. At the same time I decided to visit the Mecom Ranch, a preserve of the type just described. The King Ranch, the Y-O Ranch, and other large ranches in the South and Southwest also maintain preserves

where wild ruminants and birds of African and other origin
abound. But because on that trip I again met Luis Sanchez, game
preserve manager of the Mecom Ranch, and sat talking with him
in a coffee shop in Laredo—within sight of the International
Bridge into Mexico—I learned a lot about that particular preserve.
I'd like to discuss the wonderful thing John Mecom, has
created as a worthwhile hobby on a portion of his ranch.

The Mecom game preserve encompasses 1,500 acres fenced off
from the remainder of the ranch, a landholding of 30,000 acres.
More than fifty species of exotic game and birds are maintained in
a semiwild state on slightly less than half of the reserve's acreage.
I say semiwild, because where necessary hay, feed, and fodder are
distributed to aid the animals. Two keepers and a veterinarian are
in the residence at the ranch in order to look after the livestock
on this preserve. According to Luis Sanchez, Mr. Mecom created
the preserve some six years ago at the urging of E. Turner, now
Director of the Forest Park Zoo in Fort Worth. Among the many
species of wildlife from all over the world which thrive on the
Mecom Ranch are about 150 head of longhorn cattle. Not so
surprisingly the longhorns roam peacefully through the preserve
—without friction from their African friends. (Just as I started
a tape interview with Luis my office called. My secretary reported
that Ruhe in Hannover had sent me a telex: A cheetah due for
shipment to Montreal had been injured, had possibly broken her
leg, and what did I want to do. I immediately phoned the zoo
director in Granby, Quebec, with the news obtained and asked
his permission to delay shipment pending investigation. I phoned
my office again and had my secretary telex the instructions to
Ruhe. Imagine. There I was in Laredo, Texas, and within ten
minutes had "talked" to two countries. Contact with my office
covered 2,000 miles. My Canadian phone call covered about 2,000
miles and the back-and-forth telex with Ruhe also in Germany
traversed 6,000 miles. Approximately 10,000 miles of coordinated
communication to straighten out a problem—while my companion
leisurely puffed on his L&M.)

Springbok

Humboldt Penguins

Nubian Ibex

Llama

Saiga

Malaya Tapir

Gerenuk or Giraffe Gazelle

Bengal Tiger (*Kurt Müller*)

Defassa Waterbuck

King Penguins (*Cheyenne Mountain Zoo, Colorado Springs*)

Colobi

Sable Antelopes (*Copyright by Gerhard Dierssen*)

Mountain Gorilla

Lowland Gorilla

Walrus

Aardvark

Greater Kudu

One-day-old baby African Black Rhino

Dik Dik

Baby Cayman

Red Hartebeest

From time to time Mr. Mecom sells off excess stock to meet the needs of zoos all over the country, Luis explains: "We do not invite the public. The preserve is not a money-making proposition. It is something Mr. Mecom has done to help preserve and conserve exotic animal wildlife." And indeed he has.

Motorists driving along Route 83, south of Laredo, are often startled to see an abrupt change in the cactus-studded terrain. Suddenly they seem to be in safari country. In the distance giraffes nibble at treetops and bushes. Antelopes such as eland, oryx, impala, etc., bound gracefully across the meadow, and the ground rumbles as a herd of zebra thunders across the plain. (Mr. Mecom is conducting experiments with the eland: His interest lies in the fact that the eland, like the camel, requires very little water, and it may be possible to breed this antelope as a food source for arid countries). Suddenly Africa erupts on the Texas range. And the sight is enough to make any motorist swear off tequila forever. For me it is always a thrilling experience to visit the Mecom Ranch and see a nilgai grazing peacefully next to a longhorn, or to see zebras romping in a meadow on which buffalo placidly rest. Hunting on the preserve is strictly forbidden, because Mr. Mecom keeps his game for the enjoyment of his guests and for conservation purposes.

When guests tour the preserve they are invariably accompanied by Luis Sanchez or some other experienced person. The oryx has razor-sharp horns, and unlike most antelopes, which are timid, this noble animal can attack rather than flee when an intruder approaches. Ostriches can also be formidable, llamas too. And a scared herd of buffalo or zebra represents danger.

So if you happen to be on Route 83, south of Laredo, and if it looks like you are suddenly in Africa, remember: It isn't the tequila conjuring up the giraffes, it's Mr. Mecom. Of course there are other wild animal fanciers spread all over the world; some keep wild animal pets for their own pleasure and some maintain preserves for the pleasure of others. In any event, the fanciers all seem to have one thing in common: They are *important* people.

11.

The Red-Tape Riot

In every line of American business today the path to profits is often blocked by rules and regulations—many of them seemingly unfair and burdensome. Some rules, to put it politely, can be considered rather silly, and at times even dangerous. This is especially true to the wild animal business.

Indicative of this is the tale of my nyala.

During the night of June 3, 1969, one of my nyalas lay dying at the Clifton Quarantine Station. As soon as I was phoned about this animal's adverse condition I attempted to have a veterinarian administer antibiotics. In the past such a procedure was permissible providing the quarantine period was extended for an additional thirty days after treatment. But to my chagrin I was told that changes precluded such treatment and quarantine extension. The station spokesman bluntly told me, "It is no longer permitted." Distressed to no end I phoned the Agricuture Department's facility in Hyattsville, Maryland, and complained. An official told me in a matter-of-fact tone, "If our veterinarian administers antibiotics we may cure this animal of a quarantinable disease which we would not know about unless the animal dies."

The nyala died the following night.

Dr. Paul Lanphear of USDA and F.J. Zeehandelaar examine a Nyala after animal's death.

To me nothing is as lamentable as the sight of a dead animal —defenseless, mute, unmourned. And the sight of my dead nyala caused me to complain to the Agriculture Department.

Why?

I have always felt that the wild animals I bring in for my customers should be given the best medical care I can provide until they reach their destination. At one time the wild animal importer was permitted to have quarantined animals that became sick, treated by his own veterinarian at the quarantine installation. Now in this case, my veterinarian was not permitted to treat the nyala, a recent change, which prevented me from carrying out what I believed to be my responsibility. Still I shall persist in attempting to do everything within my power to see that defenseless wild animals imported into our country receive the best possible care at every stage of their journey, from their native habitat to their new home in the U.S.

Dr. Claude Smith, USDA, and F.J. Zeehandelaar at USDA Washington, D.C.

Bernoldt Palas and Charles Lawrence, USDI (Enforcement Branch) and F.J. Zeehandelaar at USDI Washington, D.C.

Now why do I even attempt to joust with such a powerful windmill as the Department of Agriculture? Why do I as an outdated Don Quixote, or wild animal Ralph Nader, fight for the rights of wild animals? The answer is simply I *love* the animals, and they cannot fight for themselves. If I can possibly shorten the time they must be cooped up in holding stations, quarantine stations, undersized stalls, and shipping crates, I will have won a victory for the defenseless creatures.

Thousands of American conservationists pride themselves—and rightly so—because they are involved in, or sponsor, projects dedicated to the preservation of wildlife. But few people anywhere in the world are as actively concerned about the wild animals in transit to various parts of our country—animals which perhaps suffer from archaic, insensible statutes and rulings of regulatory agencies. In this regard I have served for some years as a special advisor on animal importation to the president of the AAZPA.

And I am ready at the clichéd drop of a hat to go to bat with everything that's in me to prevent similar sad situations as the death of my nyala. Naturally there was nothing for me to do but place her carcass in Clifton's special incinerator, but maybe my complaints can forestall death for beasts in similar situations in the future.

To better understand the depth of the sea of red-tape which engulfs wild animal importation, it is fitting to dwell a bit on the rules and regulations.

First there is the agency which releases incoming shipments after all other involved agencies have approved them—the Treasury Department's U.S. Customs. This agency also collects any applicable duty.

The Public Health Service in the Department of Health, Education and Welfare must approve the importation of all primates, dogs, cats, psittacine birds, and any other kinds of animal life that could be classified as possible carriers of diseases which could infect humans.

The Agriculture Department has jurisdiction over all animals entering our country which could possibly be carriers of diseases contagious to American livestock. Such animals include equines, ruminants, swine, and all poultry. In all cases these classes of animals are subject to quarantines at terms set by this department.

The Fish and Wildlife Service of the Interior Department issues special licenses for animals subject to prohibition due to violation of internationally agreed-upon migratory acts, or regulations in the country of origin. For example, such a license would be required to import an orangutan, because the country of origin has prohibited the export of these primates.

Quite frequently the Bureau of Plant Quarantine of the Department of Agriculture gets into the wild-animal-import act, because the produce or straw bedding in the shipping crates may harbor plant diseases. And on rare occasions, when animals are shipped from Alaska to her sister states, people from the Bureau of Indian Affairs are liable to drop in on the scene for a look-see.

To the parade of official representatives from the various agencies who inspect incoming animals, we must add representatives from the ASPCA, agents of unions which control loading and unloading of planes, ships, and trucks. It is immediately apparent that animals destined for public exhibit have become quite accustomed to being stared at by humans— long before their arrivals in zoos, where they are stared at until eternity.

Rules concerning importation of some wild ruminants can become quite complex. Not only are such importations required to spend sixty days in quarantine at a foreign—and USDA approved—holding station, but, as I mentioned earlier, they must also undergo a minimum thirty-day stay at Clifton. Thereafter— and here is the rub—the perfectly disease-free animal must maintain *permanent* post-quarantine residency at an Agriculture Department *approved* zoological park, game farm, or breeding farm. The approval, of course, is on the basis of standards set by the Agriculture Department. Moreover, once a wild ruminant is in post-quarantine residency at an approved installation it cannot

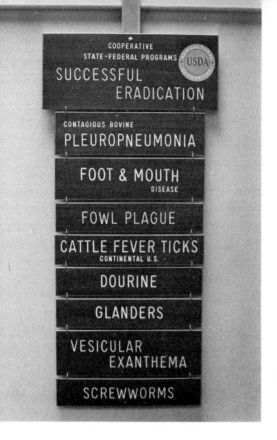

COOPERATIVE
STATE-FEDERAL PROGRAMS
USDA

SUCCESSFUL
ERADICATION

CONTAGIOUS BOVINE
PLEUROPNEUMONIA

FOOT & MOUTH
DISEASE

FOWL PLAGUE

CATTLE FEVER TICKS
CONTINENTAL U.S.

DOURINE

GLANDERS

VESICULAR
EXANTHEMA

SCREWWORMS

Plaque at USDA headquarters in Washington, D.C., lists foreign animal diseases.

be sold, swapped, or sent to any other place but an approved zoo, game, or breeding farm. For example, I have habitually turned down orders for the importation of duikers (a species of small African antelope) and chevrotains (a small Indian deer) required for research purposes by well-known institutions. Although these animals are wild ruminants and may be imported according to existing rules, I knew the USDA would not permit the entry of these needed animals because the research institutions ordering them were not USDA approved facilities.

Indeed, on several occasions I have butted my Dutch head vainly against the wall of these regulations on behalf of both universities and research institutions. In each case I have sought exceptions to the post-quarantine residency rule. And in each case I have come back with a bruised business head and the flat answer, "No."

Because the rationale of the USDA apparently is to prevent the introduction and spreading of foreign wild animal diseases I will continue to cooperate with them. But their intransigence at expanding the number of approved facilities has done nothing to expand my markets!

But as it is with so many laws, people who are enterprising soon find satisfactory solutions—legal ones, of course.

The USDA has ruled that offspring of wild ruminants residing in an approved facility may be sold and freely moved to any institution in the country: *approved* or *nonapproved.* It is for this reason that certain universities, research institutions, and unapproved game farms donate money for the importation of wild animals to an approved facility, with the proviso that offspring of the donated animals become the property of the donors.

Oddly enough, equines are not subject to the post-quarantine residency regulations and can be moved to any destination after release from the required quarantines.

Please understand: The ocean of red tape does not only lap the shores of our country. It is found elsewhere also. There are nettlesome foreign-export restrictions all over the world that can make any wild animal dealer's locks turn prematurely grey. Perhaps these restrictions arise from the frenetic efforts of tea-drinking ladies' societies that are convinced their country's animals will be cruelly treated in American zoos. And there are the more practical politicos who fear that breeding of American animal herds may reduce the export value of native foreign animals.

There are some rules that are utterly incomprehensible. Not too many years ago the Australian Government paid a bonus of several shillings for each dead wallaby, because the animals damage crops. And yet, concomitant with their payment for dead wallabys, the Australians prohibited the exportation of live ones!

Then there is the delicate question of country of origin. As previously mentioned, orangutans are prohibited by their native country to be exported. Under the new endangered species act an orangutan born outside of that country can be imported into the United States only by special permission. Certain African countries maintain lists of what they call "bona fide" zoos. And the rules of these countries prohibit the export of certain animals except to these specific zoos. How the candidates for these exclusive lists are selected has never been revealed. But I know that one of the finest—and USDA approved—zoos in the United States is not on the list, while at least two zoos, which are not USDA approved, are. This means that the African countries will not ship animals to certain USDA approved zoos and conversely the USDA will not permit imports to zoos it has not approved.

Oh well. In order to mitigate the idiosyncrasies of rules at home and abroad I often attend meetings, conferences, think sessions, and private interviews with government spokesmen here and abroad. And it is from such conferences that administrative law will someday change to benefit even more the health, welfare, and safety of wild animals in captivity, and transit.

For nineteen years I have witnessed vain attempts to eliminate the utterly nonsensical import duty on foreign livestock. Public zoos and municipal parks import animals without paying any duty. But nonpublic zoos, game farms, and importers continue to be victims of this highly selective—and biased—duty. Right now —and in the face of such pressing problems as pollution, inflation, and tight money—it doesn't seem fitting to bother our President with propaganda designed to eliminate this duty. But the assessment of a levy should be completely removed from animal imports whether for public zoos and municipal parks or not.

AGENCIES REGULATING ANIMAL IMPORTATION

DEPARTMENT OF HEALTH, EDUCATION AND WELFARE (*Public Health Service*)

1. Approves importation of all primates, dogs, cats, psittacine birds and any other kind of animal life classifiable as carriers of diseases infectious to humans.

2. Issues licenses for importation of psittacine birds (if required) and stipulates duration of quarantine of such birds.

DEPARTMENT OF THE INTERIOR (*Fish and Wildlife Service*)

1. Licenses import of animals normally on the "U.S.D.I. list of foreign endangered species."

2. Determines whether animals not on "U.S.D.I. list of foreign endangered species" have been legally exported from origin.

DEPARTMENT OF AGRICULTURE

A. *Animal Health Division*

1. Approves importation of all animals classifiable as possible carriers of diseases infectious to domestic livestock, such as equines, ruminants, swine, and poultry.

2. Stipulates duration of quarantine (if any) for certain imported animals.

B. *Plant Quarantine Division*

1. Determines whether produce, straw or other vegetable matter in imported animal shipping crates harbor plant diseases.

DEPARTMENT OF THE TREASURY (*Bureau of Customs*)

1. Admits incoming shipments (if necessary approvals from the agencies are in order.)
2. Collects import duty where applicable.

NONGOVERNMENTAL

ASPCA, labor unions controlling loading and unloading of ships, planes, trucks or other conveyances.

12.
The Factors

The financial mechanics of importing wild animals necessitate payment for the animals as soon as they are shipped, or even long before shipment. But at the same time, the importer does not receive payment until the animals have been delivered. In the case of some wild ruminants there is at least a three-month quarantine, so that the importer's capital is tied up at least for that period. In the case of dealing with municipalities, where the person who orders the animals is not the same person who writes the check, payment may be delayed as long as six months from the time the importer has laid out the primary purchase of the importation.

Because my volume of business over the past twenty years would require a multi-million-dollar capitalization on my part, I have had to resort to leverage, or credit operations. Normally when a man wants to buy a home, and he is a solid citizen, he can finance part of that home via a mortgage. In this case the bank or savings-and-loan association forecloses on the mortgaged property if the borrower defaults. But what would even the friendly Chase people do if they extended credit on an importation of a pair of rhinos and the importer defaulted? It is obvious that wild animal importations do not represent readily salable collateral —to say the least. And so in order to effect the volume of business I am accustomed to do, it was necessary to find a factor who had faith in my innate honesty and was willing to take a risk at better than going interest rates.

Fortunately most of my outside financing has come from a single source over the years. And by now these accommodating people are almost like part of my family. Officially their firm is called "The Slavenburg Corporation"; but corporations are made up of people—and these people have been exceptionally nice to me in all our business relations. And so while I want to thank everyone at Slavenburg, I especially want to express my appreciation to Han F.L. Jordan, Executive Vice-President, and to Charlotte P. Henry, Vice-President. Zoos and game farms all over the United States and Canada have been populated with exhibits because Slavenburg aided me and put up most of the money while I was waiting to be paid. Who put up the rest? I did, of course. After all I have to put some of my own capital into each and every importation, because the risks of my business rest only on my back even though the major money involved comes from my factor.

Mrs. Charlotte Henry and Mr. H. Jordan, Slavenburg Corporation, upon receipt of an Elephant figurine from F.J. Zeehandelaar.

Over the years I have been approached by people from Wall Street who wanted me to go public: i.e., sell shares in my business. And my answer invariably has been: If my business is too risky for a bank to back, why should I let the public in. Let them buy AT&T. I'll take my chances with wild animals without any help from the public.

Experience indicates, however, that financing my shipments via factors adds to the cost of the importations. This cost can be reduced in a rather simple fashion. If my customers were to pay at the time they ordered, the cost to them and to me would be reduced by the lack of the financial cost of factoring. But fat chance of that. These people from Missouri who must see the product before they pay would understandably balk at that idea. And so until some genuinely innovative approach to financing wild animal imports emerges, Zeehandelaar will continue to work with his factor.

He will also continue to cover each and every shipment with adequate insurance. The costs of insuring the animal imports adds heavily to their cost. The cost of insurance for about sixty to ninety days is roughly 30 percent of the eventual price or value of the delivered animal. In Chapter 6, I discussed the cost of importing a giraffe—from the time of capture in the jungle until delivery at a zoo in the United States. Of the total estimated $5,100 cost, the financing was only $200, but the insurance was $1,800. Upon comparison with the actual cost of the animal caught in the jungle ($1,000), it is immediately obvious that the insurance and the finance are twice what the animal itself costs to catch.

While there may be possibilities of reducing the financing costs, at this writing there do not appear to be any alternatives which permit the reduction of insurance premiums. If anything, the premiums charged on the wild animal importations must, like reverse gravity, seek their highest levels along with other inflationary trends in our economy. Percentagewise, insurance of wild animals in transit is at least 60 percent more than the Comsat company paid when it insured a recent satellite launch!

Regrettably, animals cannot be encapsulated in vinyl wrap, padded with urethane, and protected from damage during shipment. Sickness, disease, and malady peculiar to certain species may emerge at any time during transit. Changes in temperature may affect the animal adversely. The food or fodder being fed to the beast may contain disease or be harmful to digest. And there are hosts of other perfectly valid reasons for carrying insurance— including accidents which may occur when the beasts are being placed aboard or taken off ships, planes, trucks, etc.

Insuring my animals during importation is therefore part and parcel of my business. When animals die, however, the time and the trouble I spend in trying to settle the insurance claims often makes me feel like chucking the whole wild animal business and becoming a full-time writer. Additional traumas set in when an animal dies after it had already been delivered to the buyer. In some cases the buyer has not insured the animal because he thought (he says) the beast was covered by the importer's insurance. In that case the importer's bill has not been honored by the buyer and the only place one can turn to is the courts. Lawsuits are nasty long-and-drawn-out procedures which I have long ago learned to abhor, and if at all possible, avoid. But there are times in every man's life when he is convinced he is right and the other fellow is wrong. When the other fellow believes the very same thing there is nothing else to do but to go to court. Experience indicates that even when I win the court cases I come out a loser, because of the ill-will engendered. So what I usually do in almost all animal importations is insure the future exhibits for a period of thirty days beyond the anticipated delivery date. (In this regard I use Corroon & Black, specialists in covering wild animal shipments.)

This gives my customers the opportunity to decide for themselves whether or not the exhibits require insurance coverage. And if something should happen to the animal in the meantime, I am not a financial loser—and the zoo or game farm will order another animal to replace the lost one. Being human, I do not like to lose and so I advocate covering the animals despite the rather exorbitant premiums.

The animals have been caught. They have been transported safely to collecting stations. They have undergone the quarantines and the shipments without loss. The insurance company makes its profit. The factor makes his profit. The zoo has its animal. I make a piece of bread for my family. Everyone is happy.

And there is an additional, special class of humans concerned only with the welfare and the conservation of animals. These wonderful conservation people live all over the world, and because of them, wild animals may still have a very bright future despite the doleful record of extinction during the past one hundred years.

13.
The Animal Future

Demographers inundate the world today with dire predictions. We will not have any more fresh water by 1990, they warn, and we will have to drink the sea through desalination. Half the world's population will die because of starvation. Man has so destroyed his ecological balance that he will be annihiliated from his own pollution of air, water, and sewage. And on and on.

Naturally animals cannot rationalize like man does, and cannot depend upon man's largesse for survival. The intriguing question is: If man is annihilating himself, who will save the animals? That plenty of human beings care about this is patently obvious. A few years back, students and willing workers of all walks of life journeyed out from the cities into the heart of the African veldt to save thousands of baby flamingoes shackled by deathly anklets of soda ash. The clamor to save the alligator has prevented the construction of certain airport facilities in the Florida Everglades. And so it goes. While man wreaks his own destruction he is concomitantly worried about animals.

To illustrate this point in another way—animal exhibits have greatly improved during the past decade. Many parks boast what they call "African plains," areas where prides of lions roam freely and birds strut about as in their native land. The human observers stand far removed from the actual exhibit area and are separated from the exhibits by a moat (concealed or otherwise). The wild animal kingdom in captivity brings many varied species together in an ecological system. And modern zoo directors and planners are attempting to upgrade their exhibits to more nearly reflect field conditions. This was not the custom ten years ago.

But in addition to attempting to improve the method of displaying animals, and in addition to attempting to stock their zoos with greater variety of species, zoo people are well on the way to preserving species by breeding specimens in captivity. This is especially true when it comes to endangered species, or animals classified as rapidly becoming extinct.

The endangered species are:

MAMMALS

Thylacine	Hawaiian monk seal
Rusty numbat	Dugong
Leadbeater's possum	Przewalski's horse
Scaly-tailed possum	Asiatic wild ass
Broad-nosed gentle lemur	African wild ass
Mongoose lemur	Mountain zebra
Fat-tailed lemur	Central American tapir
Fork-marked mouse lemur	Great Indian rhinoceros
Western woolly avahi	Javan rhinoceros
Verreaux's sifaka	Sumatran rhinoceros
Indris	Square-lipped rhinoceros
Aye-aye	Black rhinoceros
Wooly spider monkey	Pygmy hippopotamus
Goeldi's tamarin	Wild Bactrian camel
Tana River mangabey	Persian fallow deer
Tana River red colobus	Brow-antlered deer
Orangutan	Chinese and Formosan sikas

Pygmy chimpanzee
Mountain gorilla
Ryukyu rabbit
Volcano rabbit
Kaibab squirrel
Delmarva Peninsula fox squirrel
Utah prairie dog
Block Island meadow vole
Beach meadow vole
Cuvier's hutia
Dominican hutia
Mexican grizzly bear
Polar bear
Giant panda
Black-footed ferret
Giant otter
Southern sea otter
Spanish lynx
Florida cougar
Asiatic lion
Tiger
Barbary leopard
Atlantic walrus
Ribbon seal
Ross seal
Mediterranean monk seal
Caribbean monk seal

Père David's deer
Key and Columbian
    white-tailed deer
Western giant eland
Wild Asiatic buffalo
Tamarau
Anoa
Kouprey
European bison
Wood bison
Jentink's duiker
Giant sable antelope
Arabian oryx
Scimitar-horned oryx
Addax
Bontebok
Hunter's hartebeest
Swayne's hartebeest
Black wildebeest
Beira
Slender-horned gazelle
Sumatran serow
Japanese serow
Takin
Nilgiri tahr
Walia ibex
Markhor
Cyprian mouflon

BIRDS

Giant pied-billed grebe
Short-tailed albatross
Diablotin
Cahow
Stejneger's petrel

Red-neck parrot
St. Lucia parrot
St. Vincent parrot
Prince Rupert's turaco
Red-faced malkoha

Abbott's booby
Chinese egret
Korean white stork
Giant ibis
Japanese crested ibis
Trumpeter swan
Néné
Crested shelduck
Laysan teal
Brown teal
California condor
Galápagos hawk
Hawaiian hawk
Monkey-eating eagle
Mauritius kestrel
Seychelles kestrel
La Pérouse's megapode
Pritchard's megapode
Horned guan
Prairie chicken
Western tragopan
Blyth's tragopan
Cabot's tragopan
Sclater's monal
Chinese monal
Imperial pheasant
Edwards' pheasant
Swinhoe's pheasant
White-eared pheasant
Brown-eared pheasant
Elliot's pheasant
Hume's bar-tailed pheasant
Mikado pheasant
Palawan peacock pheasant
Japanese crane
Whooping crane
Caribbean sandhill crane
Zapata rail

Seychelles owl
New Zealand laughing owl
Puerto Rico whip-poor-will
Narcondam hornbill
Okinawa woodpecker
Ivory-billed woodpecker
Imperial woodpecker
Bush wren
Small-billed false sunbird
Ruious scrub bird
Noisy scrub bird
Raza island lark
Rothschild's starling
Saddleback
Kokako
Hawaiian crow
White-breasted thrasher
Dappled bulbul
Olivaceous bulbul
Rufous-headed robin
Seychelles magpie robin
Starchy
Omao
Teita olive thrush
Grand Cayman thrush
Nihoa millerbird
Seychelles warbler
Eyrean grass wren
Chatham Island robin
Tahiti flycatcher
Tinian monarch
Seychelles paradise flycatcher
Piopio
Kauai oo
Stitchbird
Truk great white-eye
Ponapé great white-eye
Akepa

Takahé	Kauai akialoa
Kagu	Nukupuu
Great Indian bustard	Akiapolaau
New Zealand shore plover	Maui parrotbill
Eskimo curlew	Ou
Hudsonian godwit	Palila
Audouin's gull	Crested honeycreeper
Grenada dove	Bachman's warbler
Kakapo	Golden-cheeked warbler
Night parrot	Kirtland's warbler
Ground parrot	Semper's warbler
Orange-fronted kakariki	Seychelles fody
Orange-bellied parakeet	Tristan grosbeak
Beautiful parakeet	Tristan finch
Paradise parakeet	Ipswich sparrow
Puerto Rican parrot	Dusky seaside sparrow
Imperial parrot	Cape Sable seaside sparrow

No one knows at what point in man's future certain animals or birds or fish or reptiles will assume key importance. During 1969 man achieved Jules Verne's fictional dream of landing on the moon. The success of the Apollo series has conjured up visions of space travel to other planets, with space stations and space shuttles. But how many people ever stop to consider that man could never have conquered space at all if he hadn't first used monkeys? The experience gained from research on the reaction of chimpanzees to such technical phenomena as weightlessness, gravity force, etc., turned out to be vital in man's conquest of space.

Not nearly as publicized, but almost equally dramatic are experiments which will eventually permit the use of animal blood to give human blood a "rest" during heart and other major operations.

In Florida, experiments are being conducted with a certain kind of Siberian fish that eats only weeds. Three hundred of these fish are being observed in the hope that they will eat the weeds choking a certain lake. If this works, fish will aid in improving man's environment.

And so it goes. For man's own good he will have to depend upon animals in his future as he has done in his past. And for his pleasure—well, what can beat going to the park and watching an elephant curl his trunk toward his mouth to pop in peanuts or popcorn?

Indeed, in today's inflation-riddled milieu the zoos represent the greatest form of enjoyment for the least cost than almost any other form of pleasure on earth. Ironically many of the zoos in America have free days, or are without admission charges altogether. The reason this is a form of financial idiocy is that people always appreciate what they pay for and take for granted what they get for nothing. That is why I strongly advocate that zoos should charge admission at all times. Admissions, of course, would serve a twofold purpose. On the one hand the public would relish the exhibits to a greater degree, and the zoos would have additional financial resources with which to either expand their exhibits or replace specimens that age and die.

In any event, whether I wind up for the rest of my life importing new exhibit specimens or matching zoo-raised stock in order to bring buyer and seller together—it is my fullest intention to spend the rest of my days in the wacky wild animal business.

DATE DUE

GAYLORD   PRINTED IN U.S.A.